10 must-read books for women in business

Marike Fichardt 2020
www.abookamonth.club
@abookamonth_by_marike

10% of this book's profits goes to Kiva.org.
Kiva lends money to those in poor countries with no access to banking. Women can start businesses and create opportunities for themselves and their communities which would otherwise not be possible.
They are loans, not donations and 96% are repaid.
kiva.org || abookamonth.club

Dedicated to:

My fellow entrepreneurs,
freelancers, business owners.
The dreamers & doers.

Those who've been doing it for years, and those who are just dipping their toes in the water for the first time.

I see you. Doing it all. Always learning.
Riding this roller coaster.
I live this life with you.
There's nowhere else I'd rather be.

&

The authors

You're showing us the way, shining the light. Telling us your stories.
You are our teachers, our coaches and cheerleaders.

Your level of success will rarely exceed your level of personal development because success is something you attract by the person you become.

Jim Rohn

How to use this book

The book is in alphabetical title order.

For each book there is:
- a headline summary
- author detail
- a short book summary
- a reviews section

Not all the books will be right for you at all times.
Some are for beginners, others for those further along.
Some are mindset, others are tactical or strategic.
The idea is to page through, be inspired and choose what you need in order to move forward.

Important note:
I contacted each author about their summaries.
In almost all cases they have told me to use the Amazon versions their publishers .

TIP: Page through the book and follow each author on Social Media.   You will be so inspired !

A few more things

- I would love feedback - I keep revisiting the list of books, so please let me know what you are reading and your recommendations hello@abookamonth.club or @abookamonth_by_marike.

- A bit more about me: I live in the UK with my husband and 10 yo daughter.
- I own Creatures, a children's toiletries brand which I license to hotels around the world. And also soon to be the first refillable children's products available at eco and refill stores, featuring and supporting endangered animals.

- Books have changed my life, and most days you can find me reading or listening to business books while in the car, on the school run or going for a forest walk.

- I also run a friendly online book club community for female entrepreneurs.
- Find more information to join here:
- www.abookamonth.club
- IG @abookamonth_by_marike

Contents in Alphabetical Order

1 8020 Sales & Marketing - Perry Marshall

a-b

2 The Art of Saying No, Damon Zahariades
3 Ask, Ryan Levesque
4 Ask and it is Given, Esther and Jerry Hicks
5 Atomic Habits, James Clear
6 The Audacity to Be Queen, Gina deVee
7 Belong, Radha Agrawal
8 Be More Pirate, Sam Conniff Allende
9 The Big Leap, Gay Hendricks
10 Big Magic, Elizabeth Gilbert
11 Blink, Malcolm Gladwell
12 Blue Ocean Strategy, W. Chan Kim and Renée Mauborgne
13 Boss Up!, Lindsay Teague Moreno
14 The Bouncebackability Factor - Caitlin Donovan
15 Business Boutique - Christy Wright
16 But I'm Not and Expert - Meera Kothand

c-d

17 Chillpreneur - Denise Duffield-Thomas
18 The Chimp Paradox - Prof Steve Peters
19 Choose - Ryan Levque
20 Company of One - Paul Jarvis
21 The Compound Effect - Darren Hardy
22 Dare to Lead - Brene Brown
23 Daring Greatly - Brene Brown
24 Deep Work - Cal Newport
25 The Desire Map
26 Disrupt Her - Miki Agrawal
27 Do Less - Kate Northrup
28 Don't Keep Your Day Job - Cathy Heller
29 Dotcom Secrets - Russell Brunson

e-h

30 Eat that Frog - Brian Tracy
31 The E-Myth Revisited - Michael E. Gerber
32 The Entrepreneur Mind - Kevin D. Johnson
33 Essentialism - Greg McKeown
34 Everything is Figureoutable - Marie Forleo
35 Expert Secrets - Russell Brunson
36 Fear Is Not the Boss of You - Jennifer Allwood
37 The 5am Club - Robin Sharma
38 The 5 Second Rule - Mel Robbins
39 The 4-Hour Work Week - Tim Ferris
40 Get Over Your Damn Self - Romi Neustadt
41 Getting to Yes - Roger Fisher
42 Get Visible - Anna Parker-Naples
43 Get Rich Lucky Bitch - Denise Duffield-Thomas
44 #GIRLBOSS - Sophia Amoruso
45 Girl Code - Cara Alwill Leyba
46 Good Vibes Good Life - Vex King
47 The Greatest You - Trent Shelton
48 Grit - Angela Duckworth
49 The Happiness Project - Gretchen Rubin
50 High Performance Habits - Brendon Burchard
51 How to Win Friends and Influence People - Dale Carnegie
52 The $100 Start Up - Chris Guillebeau

i-l

53 Infinite Possibilities - Mike Dooley
54 Influence - Robert Cialdini
55 Influencer - Brittany Hennessy
56 The Lean Start Up - Eric Ries
57 Let It Go: A Memoir - Dame Stephanie Shirley
58 Limitless - Jim Kwik

m-r

59 Made to Stick - Chip and Dan Heath
60 Marketing Made Simple - Donald Miller
61 May Cause Miracles - Gabrielle Bernstein
62 Measure What Matters - John Doerr
63 The Million Dollar One Person Business - Elaine Pofeldt
64 Mindset - Dr Carol Dweck
65 The Miracle Morning - Hal Elrod
66 New Startup Mindset - Sandra Shpilberg
67 The One Minute Millionaire - Mark Victor Hansen
68 Outliers - Malcolm Gladwell
69 The Power of Receiving - Amanda Owen
70 Profit First - Mike Michalowicz
71 Rework - Jason Fried, David Heinemeier Hansson
72 Rocket Fuel - Gino Wickman, Mark Winters

s

73 The Science of Mind Management - Swami Mukundananda
74 Secrets of the Millionaire Mind - T. Harv Eker
75 Secrets of Six Figure Women - Barbara Stanny
76 The Seven Habits of Highly Effective People - Stephen and Sean Covey
77 She Means Business - Carrie Green
78 Shoe Dog - Phil Knight
79 Side Hustle - Chris Guillebeau
80 Slight Edge - Jeff Olson
81 Start with Why - Simon Sinek
82 Storybrand (Building a) - Donald Miller
83 The Subtle Art of Not Giving a F*ck - Mark Manson
84 The Success Principles - Jack Canfield and Janet Switzer

t-z

85 Talking to Strangers - Malcolm Gladwell
86 Think and Grow Rich - Napoleon Hill
87 Thinking Fast and Slow - Daniel Kahneman
88 Think Like a Monk - Jay Shetty
89 The Tipping Point - Malcolm Gladwell
90 Tools of Titans - Tim Ferriss
91 Traffic Secrets - Russell Brunson
92 The Ultimate Sales Machine, Chet Holmes
93 Unshakeable - Tony Robbins
94 Untamed - Glennon Doyle
95 What Got You There Won't Get You There - Marshall Goldsmith and Mark Reiter
96 What if it does work out ? Suzie Moore
97 You Are a Badass - Jen Sincero
98 You are a Badass at Making Money - Jen Sincero
99 Your Next Five Moves - Patrick Bet-David
100 Zero to One - Peter Thiel

01

8020 SALES & MARKETING

AUTHOR: PERRY MARSHALL

The Definitive Guide to Working Less and Making More

Amazon (US) star rating: 4.7 ★

Number of Amazon (US) reviews: 606

Published: 2013

About the author:
Perry Marshall is a business strategist and author.
His firm has helped small businesses become big businesses by applying the 80/20 to online advertising.
He founded the $10 million Evolution 2.0 Prize, with judges from Harvard, Oxford and MIT. Launched at the Royal Society in London, it's the world's largest science research award.
NASA's Jet Propulsion Labs uses his 80/20 Curve as a productivity tool.
His reinvention of the Pareto Principle is published in Harvard Business Review.
His Google book laid the foundations for the $100 billion Pay Per Click industry, and Ultimate Guide to Google Ads is the world's best selling book on internet advertising.
perrymarshall.com

more about
8020 SALES & MARKETING

- When you know how to walk into any situation and see the 80/20's, you can solve almost any conversion problem.

- Save 80 percent of your time and money by zeroing in on the right 20 percent of your market. By page 5 you'll be applying $80/20^2$ and $80/20^3$ to gain 10X, even 100X the success.

- With the included tools you'll see exactly how much money you're leaving on the table, and how to put it back in your pocket.

- Identify untapped markets, high-profit opportunities and incremental improvements, gaining time and greater profit potential.

- The 80/20 tool shows you big insights and invisible opportunities based on small amounts of information. See www.8020curve.com/instruction

WHAT OTHERS SAY

When you apply 80/22 pricing models, you'll never priced things the same again. Why? Because you'll understand that approximately 4% of the people who buy your product would gladly pay many times more than the asking price for a higher level of service. It's mathematically guaranteed!

You must read this book. Period. It is an easy read...very accessible, short chapters, and actually quite entertaining. Most importantly, it will revolutionize how you think about everything; it will especially open your eyes to the personal power *you* have to make your work infinitely more effective.

02
THE ART OF SAYING NO

AUTHOR: DAMON ZAHARIADES

How To Stand Your Ground, Reclaim Your Time And Energy, And Refuse To Be Taken For Granted (Without Feeling Guilty !)

Amazon (US) star rating: 4.5 ★

Number of Amazon (US) reviews: 924

Published: 2017

About the author:
Damon Zahariades covers time management strategies, review productivity apps and teach othershow to create habits to get more done while enjoying more free time.
He used to work in Corporate America and know firsthand the frustration of not being able to control his time.
Overly-long meetings, impromptu visits from coworkers and general procrastination are productivity killers.
He has authored other books on productivity topics.

artofproductivity.com

more about
THE ART OF SAYING NO

- Imagine being able to turn down requests and decline invitations with confidence and poise.
- Imagine saying no to people asking you for favors, and inspiring their respect in the process.
- A step-by-step, strategic guide for setting boundaries and developing the assertiveness you need to maintain them.
- You'll learn how to say no in every situation, at home and in the workplace, according to your convictions.
- And best of all, you'll discover how to get your friends, family members, bosses, coworkers, and neighbors to respect your boundaries and recognize your personal authority.

WHAT OTHERS SAY:

This is the easiest book I've ever read. It's definitely helpful, the most important thing is to change the way you think. Instead of feeling guilt over not helping someone, change your entire viewpoint on how valuable your own time is and what you want to do.

I found myself to be in the middle of the road on saying no. Sometimes I have no problem, others, like described in the book, guilt pressures me into saying yes - until it's burdensome. Out of fear of snapping, I picked up this book and immediately started putting these practices into action. My biggest take away from this book has been that I can't control the reactions of others.

03
ASK
AUTHOR: RYAN LEVESQUE

The Counterintuitive Online Method to Discover Exactly What Your Customers Want to Buy, Create a Mass of Raving Fans, and Take Any Business to the Next Level

Amazon (US) star rating: 4.5 ★
Number of Amazon (US) reviews: 861
Published: 2015

About the author:
Ryan Levesque is the Inc. 500 CEO of The ASK Method® Company, an entrepreneur, and the #1 national best-selling author of Ask, which was named by Inc. as the #1 Marketing Book of the Year and by Entrepreneur as the #2 Must-Read Book for Budding Entrepreneurs.
His work has been featured in the Wall Street Journal, USA Today, Forbes, and Entrepreneur, and over 250,000 entrepreneurs subscribe to his email newsletter offering business advice. .
A certified AFOL (Adult Fan of LEGO), Ryan lives with his wife, Tylene, and their two boys in Austin, Texas.

www.ryanlevesque.net   IG @askryanlevesque

more about
ASK

THE "MIND-READING" SYSTEM THAT IS REVOLUTIONIZING ONLINE BUSINESS

- Do you know how to find out what people really want to buy? (Not what you think they want, not what they say they want, but what they really want?)
- The secret is asking the right questions - and the right questions are not what you might expect.Ask is based on the compelling premise that you should NEVER have to guess what your prospects and customers are thinking.
- The Ask Formula revealed in this book has been used to help build multi-million dollar businesses in 23 different industries, generating over $100 million dollars in sales in the process.
- You 'll discover why the Ask Formula is arguably THE most powerful way to discover EXACTLY what people want to buy and how to give it to them - and in a way that makes people fall in love with you and your company.

WHAT OTHERS SAY:

"What Ryan Levesque has done is give you the art and the science behind figuring out EXACTLY what your prospects want... and then delivering it via an incredibly effective sales process. Buy this book and put the formula to work in your business - the results speak for themselves."

- Jeff Walker, #1 NY Times bestselling author of "Launch""I am going to put the brilliant advice Ryan presents in Askto work immediately. This is the most innovative, practical and useful business book I have read in years."
- Reid Tracy, CEO Hay House, Inc.

04
ASK AND IT IS GIVEN
AUTHOR: ESTHER & JERRY HICKS

Learn how to manifest your desires so that you're living the joyous and fulfilling life you deserve.

Amazon (US) star rating: 4.7 ★
Number of Amazon (US) reviews: 5,414
Published: 2004

About the authors:
Esther Hicks is an American inspirational speaker and best-selling author. She co-authored eight books with her late husband, Jerry Hicks. Together, they have presented Law of Attraction workshops in up to 60 cities per year since 1987. The Hickses' books, including the best-selling series The Law of Attraction, are – according to Esther Hicks – Channelled from a group of non-physical entities called Abraham (Hicks describes what she is doing as tapping into "infinite intelligence").
She narrated and appeared in the original version of the film The Secret, as well as being a central source of the film's inspiration.
www.abraham-hicks.com or IG @abrahamhickspublications

more about
ASK AND IT IS GIVEN

- Ask and it's Given is the teachings of the non-physical entity Abraham.
- They have drawn an extraordinary collection of endorsements from people keen to draw attention to the message that Abraham has to convey
- Understand how your relationships, health issues, finances, career concerns, and more are influenced by the Universal laws that govern your time/space reality—and you'll discover powerful processes that will help you go with the positive flow of life.
- The second half provides 22 processes you can use to get into the receiving mode and begin experiencing more joy, right now.

WHAT OTHERS SAY:

I struggled at first because this involves taking a giant leap of faith.
Left it and came back. Life altered. Incredibly.
This book changed my life.
All for the better in so many ways.

I will forever be grateful to the Hicks and all the positivity and empowerment they spread. The book is awesome and I use it a lot. Without a doubt most of what I wish for comes true too, this book just really helps you tip over the edge into believing, which is the key!

So simple, so comforting, so enjoyable to read. As you turn each page you wonder how you could ever have made such a tangled mess of your life when it all appears so easy to have an enjoyable life

05
ATOMIC HABITS
AUTHOR: JAMES CLEAR

TINY CHANGES, REMARKABLE RESULTS
An Easy and Proven Way to Build Good Habits and Break Bad Ones

Amazon (US) star rating: 4.8 ★

Number of Amazon (US) reviews: 15,669

Published: 2018

About the author
James Clear is an expert on habits and decision making. He made his name as the author of one of the fastest-growing email newsletters in history, which grew from zero to 100,000 subscribers in under two years.
Today, his newsletter has over 650,000 subscribers, and his articles receive 10 million hits each year.

www.jamesclear.com   IG: @jamesclear

more about
ATOMIC HABITS

- People think when you want to change your life, you need to think big.
- But world-renowned habits expert James Clear has discovered another way.
- He knows that real change comes from the compound effect of hundreds of small decisions doing two push-ups a day, waking up five minutes early, or holding a single short phone call.
- There's a good amount of additional supporting material that you can download too (links are in the book).
- So you not only get the book to read, but lots of extras to help you make use of what is taught.

WHAT OTHERS SAY:

This book is different from others in the way it covers an enormous amount of ground in the larger area of self-improvement while seamlessly tying all these ideas back into the central theme of habits.

His one article has absolutely changed my life, imagine what this book can offer to you.

James Clear has a great writing style which captures you and makes it easy to grasp his teaching. I've had so many eureka moments and realisations reading the blog and look forward to finishing this wonderful book.

06
THE AUDACITY TO BE QUEEN

AUTHOR: GINA DEVEE

The Unapologetic Art of Dreaming Big and Manifesting Your Most Fabulous Life

Amazon US star rating: 4.7 ★

Number of Amazon US reviews: 170 (newcomer)

Published 2020

About the author:

Gina's DeVee's journey from struggling psychotherapist (who lived at home with her parents) to globetrotting entrepreneur has led her to founding her multi-million dollar women's empowerment company, Divine Living.

Divine Living is for the woman who's excited about impacting the world; craves a spiritual connection, dares to be visible, and desires to fulfill her life's purpose.

Gina is an author, speaker, podcast host and success coach. She has dedicated her career to helping clients connect spiritually, start businesses, create wealth and live life to the fullest.
www.divineliving.com   IG @ginadevee

more about

THE AUDACITY TO BE QUEEN

- Gina invites modern-day women to take ourselves off the back-burner financially, romantically, physically, and socially. With illuminating stories, steps, prayers and journal prompts, she shows us how to:
- Reclaim our femininity & manifest our deepest desires
- Develop unshakeable spiritual confidence & complete clarity on our big career moves
- Make, invest & enjoy money
- And release any self-doubt or self-sabotage so that we can be seen and recognized for our highest talents

WHAT OTHERS SAY:

Gina DeVee is a master at articulating what it means to be an empowered woman. This book is the guide we've been waiting for. Get ready y'all, the Queens have arrived! **Jen Sincero**

"In a world celebrating the rise of the feminine, Gina's timely & unapologetic message models for women what it means to be empowered, prioritized and spiritually connected in our modern era."- Marianne Williamson

I just finished this book and it was so amazing. I am going back and rereading with a fine tooth comb. But this time I will be wearing my crown and not my peasant dress.

07
BELONG

AUTHOR: RADHA AGRAWAL

Find Your People, Create Community, and Live a More Connected Life

Amazon (US) star rating: 4.7 ★

Number of Amazon (US) reviews: 184

Published: 2018

About the author:

Radha is a successful social entrepreneur, impact investor, inventor, speaker, and lifelong community builder.
She founded Daybreaker, the grassroots, sober early-morning dance phenomenon.
Radha is also an angel investor with over a dozen exciting start-ups.
She travels around the world speaking on social entrepreneurship and community building.

radhaagrawal.com IG: @love.radha

more about BELONG

- How is it that the internet connects us to a world of people, yet so many of us feel more isolated than ever?
- Radha Agrawal calls this "community confusion," and she offers every reader a blueprint to find their people and build and nurture community, because connectedness—as more and more studies show—is our key to happiness, fulfilment, and success.
- A book that's equal parts inspiring and interactive, and packed with prompts, charts, quizzes, and full-color illustrations, Belong takes readers on a two-part journey. GOING IN and GOING OUT.

WHAT OTHERS SAY:

If you want to belong, read this book. Deepak Chopra, M.D.

From the moment I opened this book I was hooked. Radha is that friend whispering in your ear, assuring you that not only does she understand your feelings of loneliness and your wish to belong, she'll also take you gently but firmly by the hand to act, to connect, to create purpose, and to build your community. This book is caring and tender, challenging and action-driven.
Esther Perel

Ever felt like you haven't quite found your community yet, the place where you can fully flourish as the best possible version of you? No need to wait anymore. In "Belong", Radha Agrawal shows you how you roll your own.

08
BE MORE PIRATE
AUTHOR: SAM CONNIFF ALLENDE
How to Take on
the World and Win

Amazon (US) star rating: 4.5 ★
Number of Amazon (US) reviews: 178
Published: 2018

About the author:
Sam Conniff Allende is the founder and former CEO of Livity, a multi-award-winning youth marketing agency.
Sam has led the unlikeliest collaborations between brands and bright young people on the edges of society, resulting in real innovation.
He has worked with Google, Unilever, PlayStation, and Dyson, and regularly speaks and runs Be More Pirate workshops at these industry-leading companies.
Sam handed over the Captain's Hat to Alex Barker, the woman who'd been his Community Manager the last two years to co-author the sequel How to: Be More Pirate (out now) based on all the rebellions the first book inspired (with a majority of the case studies being women).
Alex is now the head of the Global Community deciding where to take Be More Pirate next.
samconniff.com   IG @samconniff

more about
BE MORE PIRATE

- "I'd rather be a pirate than join the navy."—Steve Jobs
- Whatever your ambitions, ideas and challenges, Be More Pirate will revolutionize the way you live, think, and work today, and tomorrow. So what are you waiting for?
- Be More Pirate unveils the innovative strategies of Golden Age pirates, drawing parallels between the tactics and teachings of legends like Henry Morgan and Blackbeard with modern rebels, like Elon Musk, Malala, and Banksy.
- Featuring takeaway sections and a guide to building your own pirate code 2.0, Be More Pirate will show you how to leave your mark on the 21st century.
- Join the rebellion ?

WHAT OTHERS SAY:

A model for how to break the system and create radical change.
Evening Standard.
This isn't a book, it's the beginning of a movement. Be More Pirate should come with a health warning. Tom Goodwin, author

Learn to become a warrior for your own cause.

How to innovate for the future... Be More Pirate! This author has done a great job of making me think outside the box in business and try things a different way.

09
THE BIG LEAP
AUTHOR: GAY HENDRICKS

Conquer your hidden fear, and take life to the next level.

Amazon (US) star rating: 4.6 ★

Number of Amazon (US) reviews: 1,876

Published: 2009

About the author:

Gay Hendricks is the author and coauthor of more than twenty books that deal with personal growth, including the New York Times bestseller Five Wishes and Conscious Living.

Throughout his career, he has coached more than eight hundred executives, including the top management at firms such as Dell, Hewlett-Packard, Motorola, and KLM.

Along with his wife, Dr. Kathlyn Hendricks, he has coauthored many books including Conscious Loving, The Corporate Mystic, and his latest, the New York Times bestseller Five Wishes, which has been translated into seventeen languages.

After a twenty-one-year career as a professor at the University of Colorado, he founded the Hendricks Institute, which offers seminars in North America, Asia, and Europe. He is also a founder of The Spiritual Cinema Circle.

hendricks.com

more about
THE BIG LEAP

- Most of us believe that we will finally feel satisfied and content with our lives when we get the good news we have been waiting for, find a healthy relationship, or achieve one of our personal goals. However, this rarely happens.
- Good fortune is often followed by negative emotions that overtake us and result in destructive behaviors. "I don't deserve this," "this is too good to be true," or any number of harmful thought patterns prevent us from experiencing the joy and satisfaction we have earned. Sound familiar?
- This is what Gay Hendricks calls the Upper Limit Problem, a negative emotional reaction that occurs when anything positive enters our lives.
- The Upper Limit Problem not only prevents happiness, but it actually stops us from achieving our goals. It is the ultimate life roadblock.

WHAT OTHERS SAY:

*You know, it's rare, when you're a colossal nerd who reads literally everything you can get your hands on,
to find a book that is somewhat lifechanging.*

If you're on the path of self-discovery and self-transformation, don't wait, GET THIS BOOK! Just in the course of reading the first few pages I felt like I was rearranging my perception of my self, of life, and of what I'm capable of creating and experiencing with the time I have on this planet.

I find myself referencing it mentally at the most miserable of moments … and choosing different responses. It has been life changing to me - on content alone. And I've sent copies to most of my extended family over the past couple of years too.

10
BIG MAGIC

AUTHORS: ELIZABETH GILBERT

Creative Living Beyond Fear

Amazon (US) star rating: 4.6 ★

Number of Amazon (US) reviews: 5,640

Published: 2016

About the author:

Elizabeth Gilbert is the #1 New York Times bestselling author of Big Magic, Eat Pray Love, and The Signature of All Things, as well as several other internationally bestselling books of fiction and nonfiction.

Elizabeth divides her time between New York City, rural New Jersey, and everywhere else.

elizabethgilbert.com   IG @elizabeth_gilbert_writer

more about
BIG MAGIC

- Readers of all ages and walks of life have drawn inspiration and empowerment from Elizabeth Gilbert's books for years.
- Now this beloved author digs deep into her own generative process to share her wisdom and unique perspective about creativity.
- With profound empathy and radiant generosity, she offers potent insights into the mysterious nature of inspiration.
- She asks us to embrace our curiosity and let go of needless suffering. She shows us how to tackle what we most love, and how to face down what we most fear.
- She discusses the attitudes, approaches, and habits we need in order to live our most creative lives.
- Gilbert encourages us to uncover the "strange jewels" that are hidden within each of us.
- Whether we are looking to write a book, make art, find new ways to address challenges in our work, embark on a dream long deferred, or simply infuse our everyday lives with more mindfulness and passion,

WHAT OTHERS SAY

"A must read for anyone hoping to live a creative life... I dare you not to be inspired to be brave, to be free, and to be curious." — PopSugar

"Gilbert demystifies the creative process, examining the practices of great artists to shed light on finding inspiration in the every day." —Harper's Bazaar

Thank you Liz, this book found me in just the perfect moment. It has irritated, needled, stroked and cajoled my ideas about my own creative process. But more than anything it has been the kick in the pants I needed to get back to work.

11
BLINK
AUTHOR: MALCOLM GLADWELL

The Power of Thinking
without Thinking

Amazon (US) star rating: 4.5 ★
Number of Amazon (US) reviews: 4,918
Published: 2007

About the author:

Malcolm Gladwell is the author of five New York Times bestsellers —
The Tipping Point, Blink, Outliers, What the Dog Saw, and David and
Goliath.

He is also the co-founder of Pushkin Industries, an audio content
company that produces the podcasts Revisionist History, which
reconsiders things both overlooked and misunderstood, and Broken
Record, where he, Rick Rubin, and Bruce Headlam interview musicians
across a wide range of genres.
Gladwell has been included in the TIME 100 Most Influential People
list and touted as one of Foreign Policy's Top Global Thinkers.

gladwellbooks.com IG @malcolmgladwell

more about
BLINK

- Blink is a book about how we think without thinking, about choices that seem to be made in an instant-in the blink of an eye-that actually aren't as simple as they seem.
- Why do some people follow their instincts and win, while others end up stumbling into error?
- How do our brains really work-in the office, in the classroom, in the kitchen, and in the bedroom?
- And why are the best decisions often those that are impossible to explain to others?
- In Blink we meet the psychologist who has learned to predict whether a marriage will last, based on a few minutes of observing a couple; the tennis coach who knows when a player will double-fault before the racket even makes contact with the ball.
- Blink reveals that great decision makers aren't those who process the most information or spend the most time deliberating, but those who have perfected the art of "thin-slicing"-filtering the very few factors that matter from an overwhelming number of variables.

WHAT OTHERS SAY:

This is an incredible tour de force with detailed research and eye-opening, and often disheartening insights into our flawed personal decision making processes.

Mind-blowing! Truly a fantastic read and I feel like I learned a lot about how different types of thinking give us better results in different scenarios.

12
BLUE OCEAN STRATEGY

AUTHOR: W CHAN KIM & RENEE MAUBORGNE

How to Create Uncontested Market Space and Make the Competition Irrelevant

Amazon (US) star rating: 4.5 ★
Number of Amazon (US) reviews: 1,843
Published 2015

About the authors:

Chan Kim and Renée Mauborgne are Professors of Strategy at INSEAD, one of the world's top business schools, and co-directors of the INSEAD Blue Ocean Strategy Institute in Fontainebleau, France.

In 2019, Named the #1 Management Thinkers in the World by Thinkers50.
Blue Ocean Strategy, which is published in 46 languages, has hit more than 300 bestseller lists across the globe and has received numerous distinguished awards

blueoceanstrategy.com

more about
BLUE OCEAN STRATEGY

- Blue oceans strategy is the approach that suggests a company is better off searching for ways to play in uncontested market places instead of engaging with competition in existing marketing spaces.
- It is the idea of trying to find market spaces that are free of competitors by creating and caputuring new demand, making the competition irrelevant.
- Netflix created uncontested marketing space by selling TV shows over the internet which no one else was currently doing. By doing this they made the competition irrelevant, creating and capture new demand for a service not currently available on the market.
- By entering a blue ocean they were able to pursue low cost and differentiation leadership compared to the alternatives to their product.
- Other examples are Apple, Nintendo, Cirque du Soleil The Home Depot, and many more
- Blue Oceans lead to easy growth because there is no competition- using a blue ocean strategy has an incredibly high return on investment.

WHAT OTHERS SAY
"One of the bestselling business books of the century"
Financial Times

What this book does best is give you a formula to think about things you may not have considered in your drive to compete with others in your space.

13
BOSS UP !
LINDSAY TEAGUE MORENO

This Ain't Your Mama's Business Book. Put your business on the map and the ideas you've previously only dreamed about into the marketplace.

Amazon (US) star rating: 4.8 ★
Number of Amazon (US) reviews: 537
Published:2019

About the author:

Lindsay Teague Moreno is an entrepreneur, author, speaker and podcaster (The Boss Up).
In just two short years she built a seven-figure personal income, using only social media.
She did this with three little girls at home and all the mom duties that come along with it.
Raising businesses and babies at the same time is no easy feat, but anything is possible if you have enough dry shampoo and grit.

lindsaytm.com IG: lindsayteague

more about
BOSS UP !

- In Boss Up! Lindsay helps you gain the confidence to know that having ambition doesn't make you a bad mother or wife.
- That it's okay to have a desire for something more than endless sippy cups, clean-ups, Band-Aids, and groundings.
- That no matter your education or experience, you can tap into your passions and create businesses that give you increased flexibility, fulfillment, and financial security.
- Using the lessons she learned on her own path to success, Lindsay shares real, solid business principles with ten distinct success philosophies that you will encounter on the journey to entrepreneurship

WHAT OTHERS SAY:

"Lindsay Teague Moreno is a no-fluff, no-fear leader for entrepreneurs. This book is the perfect guide to starting a business and fulfilling your dreams." John C Maxwell #1 NY Times bestselling author, world-renowned leadership expert

"If I ever need someone to kick my butt, supercharge my creativity, or call me out on something silly I'm doing in my business, Lindsay is who I reach out to."

"Get ready. You're about to meet one of my favorite business leaders ever. And if you do even 10 percent of what this book suggests, things are about to grow for your business in the best possible way."
Jon Acuff, NY Times bestselling author

THE *14* BOUNCEBACKBALITY FACTOR

AUTHOR: CAITLIN DONOVAN

End Burnout, Gain Resilience, and Change the World

Amazon US star rating: 5 ★

Number of Amazon US reviews: 22 (newcomer)

Published: 2020

More about the author:

Caitlin Donovan is one of New York City's leading burnout experts and acupuncturists, host of "Fried - The Burnout Podcast," and author of the book "The Bouncebackability Factor: End Burnout, Gain Resilience, and Change the World".

Her master's degree in Traditional Chinese Medicine enables Caitlin to combine Eastern wisdom with her natural practicality.

After performing more than 25,000 acupuncture treatments,, Caitlin added 1:1 coaching, corporate workshops, and keynotes for companies such as PTC and Lululemon - all with a focus on burnout.

caitdonovan.com friedtheburnoutpodcast.com
IG @cait_donovan

more about
THE BOUNCEBACKBALITY FACTOR

- This is a book for everyone who has ever felt FRIED with a special focus on the female entrepreneur.
- In a world where women are told that they can have it all and be it all, the high achievers are looking down from the top of the mountain and wondering why it doesn't feel as good as they thought it might.
- As opposed to focusing on the workplace, increasing positivity, leaning in even more, or productivity measures, The Bouncebackability Factor zooms in on the REAL reasons burnout is so rampant and what every individual can do to end their own personal burnout culture in order to reclaim energy, joy, and fulfillment.
- The Bouncebackability Factor offers the reader 7 major burnout causes and their fixes.
- The main message: Burnout is NOT your fault. This book will prove that to you all while holding your hand and guiding you toward healing, no matter which cause of burnout is most prevalent in your life.

WHAT OTHERS SAY:
I had SO many lightbulb moments reading this book! In fact, I think I highlighted more paragraphs than I didn't! The biggest lightbulb moment I think was about past trauma living in the body and how that contributes to chronic stress.

Demystifying burnout. Burnout has been an ever-present challenge throughout my life. Hell, I seem to have invented the phenomenon. Or at least perfected it. As such it was beautiful to read Cait's book. It talks in open and honest words about the causes and manifestations of burnout, before guiding the reader towards solutions and further reading.

15
BUSINESS BOUTIQUE

AUTHOR: CHRISTY WRIGHT

A Woman's Guide for Making Money Doing What She Loves

Amazon (US) star rating: 4.5 ★
Number of Amazon (US) reviews: 694
Published: 2017

About the author:

Both entertaining and inspiring, Christy Wright is a Certified Business Coach and Ramsey Personality who presents messages that educate and give hope to audiences nationwide.
As the creator of Business Boutique and through her podcast and sellout live events,. she uses her experience as an entrepreneur and leader to connect with women and give them practical advice and solutions for their personal and professional development.
She has touched the lives of many with her inspiring and thought-provoking messages on topics including life balance, leadership and goal setting.
She and her husband, Matt, live in Brentwood, Tennessee, with their 3 children.

christywright.com IG @ChristyBWright

more about
BUSINESS BOUTIQUE

- Business Boutique is a life-changing handbook from the heart of Christy Wright, creator of the Business Boutique movement.
- It offers a step-by-step plan to take the ideas in your head and turn them into a business that brings some serious income.
- Stop treating your desires and gifts like an afterthought and start chasing your dreams! Business Boutique will show you how to:
- Create a customized plan to start and grow your business
- Manage your time so you can have a business—and life—you love
- Simplify the overwhelming business stuff like pricing, taxes and budgeting
- Market to the right people the right way
- Sell with confidence

WHAT OTHERS SAY:

If you're a lost woman in the small business world ... READ this!!!!
I felt like I was falling behind in a lot of the "business" side of my small business but, after reading this I feel more confident and empowered in my ability to make my small business a success!
Christy's writing style has a knowledgeable "big sister" feel.

Christy provides some great insight on how to create a business that feeds your soul and feeds your bank account! I am going to read it again because it is full of great ideas and valuable lessons!

Christy breaks it all down to make it easy to pull together your business plan.

16

BUT I'M NOT AN EXPERT

AUTHOR: MEERA KOTHAND

Go from newbie to expert and radically skyrocket your influence without feeling like a fraud

Amazon (US) star rating: 4.5 ★
Number of Amazon (US) reviews: 159
Published: 2018

About the author:

Meera Kothand is an email marketing strategist and 3 times Amazon best-selling author of the books The One Hour Content Plan, But I'm not an Expert & Your First 100.

Using her unique Profitable Email System™ and ADDictive Business Framework, she makes powerful marketing strategies simple and relatable so that small business owners can build a tribe that's addicted to their zone of genius.

meerakothand.com IG @meerakothand

more about
BUT I'M NOTAN EXPERT

- How are some solopreneurs able to command attention?
- How do some become experts, while others fade into the background as simply white noise?
- How do you stop feeling like an imposter or fraud when you might as well be this tiny speck among the thousands of online businesses out there?
- If you've ever said the words "But I'm not an expert!" this book is for you.
- This book will address the fears of thousands of newbies struggling to build an influence online.
- You don't have to fake it or feel like a fraud. The strategies and hacks you'll discover are not gimmicks or secrets. These are intentional, calculated steps that you can take to get there.

WHAT OTHERS SAY:

If you feel overwhelmed by all the things you've read and all the content you've consumed on how to position your brand/your barely-off-the-ground business, all the must-do-this-must-do-that of the online world … take a deep breath, click the Buy Now button and just devour this gem by Meera.

I stumbled across Meera late one night and I'm so thankful that I did. She has changed the game for me.
I found the book to be ACTIONABLE, not just full of theory.

Meera has an epic talent of taking overwhelming aspects of building an online business and breaking it down into the simplest, actionable steps. This book was just lightbulb moment after lightbulb moment!

17
CHILLPRENEUR

AUTHOR: DENISE DUFFIELD THOMAS

The New Rules for Creating Success, Freedom, and Abundance on Your Terms

Amazon (US) star rating: 4.8 ★
Number of Amazon (US) reviews: 220
Published: 2019

About the author:
Denise Duffield-Thomas is the money mindset mentor for the new wave of online female entrepreneurs.

Her best-selling books "Lucky Bitch" and "Get Rich, Lucky Bitch" give a fresh and funny road-map to create an outrageously successful life and business.

Denise helps women release their fear of money, set premium prices for their services and take back control over their finances.

Denise is an award winning speaker, author and entrepreneur who helps women transform their Economy-Class money mindset into a First-Class life.

LuckyBitch.com   IG: @denisedt

more about
CHILLPRENEUR

- Feeling burned out by your business? Sick of the "hustle and grind" culture of your industry?
- There's a better way!
- Get over your perfectionism and embrace the flow of the chillpreneur.
- Denise will show you how with her trademark humor and down-to-earth wisdom.
- In this book, she shares invaluable business advice and counter-intuitive millionaire mindset lessons (no blood, sweat, or tears necessary) which will set you on the path of abundance - without all the hard work.
- You'll discover how to find the business model that works perfectly for your personality, learn about key concepts to help you work less and earn more, and become a marketing pro without feeling like a sleazy car salesman.
- Full of reassuring and practical advice, Chillpreneur challenges the old, boring assumptions of what it takes to create success in business, so you can create financial independence with ease and grace.

WHAT OTHERS SAY:

'Denise Duffield-Thomas [is] one of the foremost financial advisors for females.' Entrepreneur.com

'Denise is one of the most honest, transparent, unapologetic voices out there leading women to prosperity.
Her work is so important.'
Kate Northrup, author of Money, A Love Story

18
THE CHIMP PARADOX

AUTHOR: PROF STEVE PETERS

The Mind Management Program to Help You Achieve Success, Confidence, and Happiness

Amazon (US) star rating: 4.5 ★
Number of Amazon (US) reviews: 5,806
Published: 2013

About the author:

Dr. Steve Peters is a Consultant Psychiatrist who specializes in optimizing the functioning of the mind.

He is Undergraduate Dean at Sheffield University Medical School and the resident psychiatrist with the British Cycling and Sky ProCycling teams.

chimpmanagement.com

more about
THE CHIMP PARADOX

- Your inner Chimp can be your best friend or your worst enemy...this is the Chimp Paradox.
- Do you sabotage your own happiness and success?
- Are you struggling to make sense of yourself?
- Do your emotions sometimes dictate your life?
- Dr. Steve Peters explains that we all have a being within our minds that can wreak havoc on every aspect of our lives—be it business or personal.
- He calls this being "the chimp," and it can work either for you or against you. The challenge comes when we try to tame the chimp, and persuade it to do our bidding.
- This book will help you to:
- —Recognize how your mind is working
- —Understand and manage your emotions and thoughts
- —Manage yourself and become the person you would like to be
- Dr. Peters explains the struggle that takes place within your mind and then shows you how to apply this understanding.
- Once you're armed with this new knowledge, you will be able to utilize your chimp for good, rather than letting your chimp run rampant with its own agenda.

WHAT OTHERS SAY:

"Thank you, Steve Peters, for opening my eyes on how to approach my worries and fears..." Bradley Wiggins, Winner Tour de France 2012
'This mind program that helped me win my Olympic Golds." Sir Chris Hoy, 6-time Olympic champion

This book has helped me so much in EVERY ASPECT of my life, time and time again.
This is by far the best book I have ever read to explain all the "chatter" in ones head.

19
CHOOSE
AUTHOR: RYAN LEVESQUE

The Single Most Important Decision Before Starting Your Business

Amazon (US) star rating: 4.5 ★

Number of Amazon (US) reviews: 204

Published: 2019

About the author:

Ryan Levesque is the Inc. 500 CEO of The ASK Method® Company, an entrepreneur, and the #1 national best-selling author of Ask, which was named by Inc. as the #1 Marketing Book of the Year and by Entrepreneur as the #2 Must-Read Book for Budding Entrepreneurs. His work has been featured in the Wall Street Journal, USA Today, Forbes, and Entrepreneur, and over 250,000 entrepreneurs subscribe to his email newsletter offering business advice. .
A certified AFOL (Adult Fan of LEGO), Ryan lives with his wife, Tylene, and their two boys in Austin, Texas.

www.ryanlevesque.net   IG @askryanlevesque

more about
CHOOSE

- One of the biggest reasons why so many new businesses fail is because in the quest to decide what business to start, most of the conventional wisdom is wrong.
- Instead of obsessing over what - as in what should you sell or what should you build - you should first be asking who. As in who should you serve?
- The what is a logical question that will come soon enough. But choosing your who is the foundation from which all other things are built.
- That is what this book is all about. If you've ever had the dream to start your own business, become your own boss, or do your own thing- but have been afraid to take the leap and screw up your already good life - this book is for you.
- You will find the meticulously tested, step-by-step process outlined in the book is easy to follow, despite being the result of a decade of research and experience.
- This process, designed to minimize your risk of failure and losing money up front, coupled with the inspiring stories of everyday people who have used this process to launch successful businesses, will not only give you clarity on what type of business to start, but also the confidence to finally take that leap and get started.

WHAT OTHERS SAY:

"Starting a business may be the riskiest thing you'll ever do. Ryan Levesque cuts the risk down to size, helping you make the single, biggest choice you face: selecting the right market."
– Michael Hyatt, NY Times best-selling author of Your Best Year Ever

20

COMPANY OF ONE

AUTHOR: PAUL JARVIS

Why Staying Small
Is the Next Big

Amazon (US) star rating: 4.6 ★
Number of Amazon (US) reviews: 330
Published: 2019

About the author:

Paul Jarvis is a writer, a designer, a podcaster, an online course teacher, and software creator.
He spent years working with professional athletes like Warren Sapp, Steve Nash and Shaquille O'Neal with their online presence, and with large companies like Yahoo, Microsoft, Mercedes-Benz and Warner Music.
He then migrated to working with online entrepreneurs like Marie Forleo, Danielle LaPorte, and Kris Carr to help build their brands.
Since becoming a company of one, he spends his time writing, podcasting, and creating online courses for more than 15,000 students, which has been translated into 18 languages.
He lives with his wife on an island off the coast of Vancouver.

www.ofone.co

more about
COMPANY OF ONE

- What if the real key to a richer and more fulfilling career was not to create and scale a new start-up, but rather, to be able to work for yourself, determine your own hours, and become a (highly profitable) and sustainable company of one?
- Suppose the better—and smarter—solution is simply to remain small? This book explains how to do just that.
- Company of One is a refreshingly new approach centered on staying small and avoiding growth, for any size business.
- Not as a freelancer who only gets paid on a per piece basis, and not as an entrepreneurial start-up that wants to scale as soon as possible, but as a small business that is deliberately committed to staying that way.
- By staying small, one can have freedom to pursue more meaningful pleasures in life, and avoid the headaches that result from dealing with employees, long meetings, or worrying about expansion.
- Company of One introduces this unique business strategy and explains how to make it work for you, including how to generate cash flow on an ongoing basis.

WHAT OTHERS SAY:
"Jarvis makes a compelling case for making your business better instead of bigger. A must-read for any entrepreneur who prioritizes a rich life over riches."

—CAL NEWPORT, bestselling author of DEEP WORK and DIGITAL MINIMALISM

21

THE COMPOUND EFFECT

AUTHOR: DARREN HARDY

Multiply Your Success One Simple Step at a Time

Amazon (US) star rating: 4.8 ★

Number of Amazon (US) reviews: 4,915

Published: 2011

About the author:

Darren Hardy has been the central business leader of the success media industry for over 25 years.

More than anyone alive today, Darren has met, interviewed and uncovered the methods used by the most successful people in the world.

He now teaches these unique success strategies exclusively to those who choose to...Be The Exception

darrenhardy.com

more about
THE COMPOUND EFFECT

- This book reveals the core principles that drive success.
- The Compound Effect contains the essence of what every superachiever needs to know, practice, and master to obtain extraordinary success. Inside you will find strategies on:
- The No. 1 strategy to achieve any goal and triumph over any competitor, even if they're smarter, more talented or more experienced.
- Eradicating your bad habits (some you might be unaware of!) that are derailing your progress.
- Painlessly installing the few key disciplines required for major breakthroughs.
- The real, lasting keys to motivation--how to get yourself to do things you don't feel like doing.
- Capturing the elusive, awesome force of momentum.
- The acceleration secrets of superachievers. Do they have an unfair advantage? Yes, they do, and now you can too!

WHAT OTHERS SAY:
It really helped me to do something that I've struggled with for years. It helped me to develop a plan to make improvements in my life.
I've read many works on personal development but I've never been able to fully implement ideas or methods.

This book is so good I find myself reaching for it again and again when I need motivation.

22
DARE TO LEAD
AUTHOR: BRENE BROWN

Brave Work.
Tough Conversations.
Whole Hearts.

Amazon (US) star rating: 4.7 ★

Number of Amazon (US) reviews: 5,523

Published: 2018

About the author:

Brené Brown, PhD, LMSW, is a research professor at the University of Houston, where she holds the Huffington Foundation-Brené Brown Endowed Chair at the Graduate College of Social Work.

She has spent the past two decades studying courage, vulnerability, shame, and empathy and is the author of four #1 New York Times bestsellers: Braving the Wilderness, Rising Strong, Daring Greatly, and The Gifts of Imperfection.

Her TED talk—"The Power of Vulnerability"—is one of the top five most-viewed TED talks in the world with more than thirty-five million views.

Brene lives in Houston, Texas, with her husband, Steve, and their children, Ellen and Charlie.

brenebrown.com   IG @brenebrown

more about
DARE TO LEAD

- Leadership is not about titles, status, and wielding power.
- A leader is anyone who takes responsibility for recognizing the potential in people and ideas, and has the courage to develop that potential.
- When we dare to lead, we don't pretend to have the right answers; we stay curious and ask the right questions. We don't see power as finite and hoard it; we know that power becomes infinite when we share it with others. We don't avoid difficult conversations and situations; we lean into vulnerability when it's necessary to do good work.
- But daring leadership in a culture defined by scarcity, fear, and uncertainty requires skill-building around traits that are deeply and uniquely human.
- The irony is that we're choosing not to invest in developing the hearts and minds of leaders at the exact same time as we're scrambling to figure out what we have to offer that machines and AI can't do better and faster.
- What can we do better? Empathy, connection, and courage, to start.
- Don't miss the Netflix special - Brené Brown: The Call to Courage!

WHAT OTHERS SAY:

"Whether you're leading a movement or a start-up, if you're trying to change an organizational culture or the world, Dare to Lead will challenge everything you think you know about brave leadership and give you honest, straightforward, actionable tools for choosing courage over comfort."—Tarana Burke, senior director, Girls for Gender Equity, founder, the Me Too movement

It highlights the amazing opportunity we all have to create joy and fairness in our workspaces and our relationships.

23
DARING GREATLY
AUTHOR: BRENE BROWN
How the Courage to Be Vulnerable Transforms the Way We Live, Love, Parent, and Lead

Amazon (US) star rating: 4.8 ★
Number of Amazon (US) reviews: 5,445
Published: 2015

About the author:

Brené Brown, PhD, LMSW, is a research professor at the University of Houston, where she holds the Huffington Foundation-Brené Brown Endowed Chair at the Graduate College of Social Work.

She has spent the past two decades studying courage, vulnerability, shame, and empathy and is the author of four #1 New York Times bestsellers: Braving the Wilderness, Rising Strong, Daring Greatly, and The Gifts of Imperfection.

Her TED talk—"The Power of Vulnerability"—is one of the top five most-viewed TED talks in the world with more than thirty-five million views.

Brene lives in Houston, Texas, with her husband, Steve, and their children, Ellen and Charlie.
brenebrown.com IG @brenebrown

more about
DARING GREATLY

- Every day we experience the uncertainty, risks, and emotional exposure that define what it means to be vulnerable or to dare greatly.
- Based on twelve years of pioneering research, Brené Brown PhD, LMSW, dispels the cultural myth that vulnerability is weakness and argues that it is, in truth, our most accurate measure of courage.
- Daring Greatly is not about winning or losing. It's about courage.
- In a world where "never enough" dominates and feeling afraid has become second nature, vulnerability is subversive. Uncomfortable. It's even a little dangerous at times.
- And, without question, putting ourselves out there means there's a far greater risk of getting criticized or feeling hurt.
- But when we step back and examine our lives, we will find that nothing is as uncomfortable, dangerous, and hurtful as standing on the outside of our lives looking in and wondering what it would be like if we had the courage to step into the arena—whether it's a new relationship, an important meeting, the creative process, or a difficult family conversation.
- Daring Greatly is a practice and a powerful new vision for letting ourselves be seen.

WHAT OTHERS SAY:
What I find remarkable about this book is the unique combination of solid research and kitchen table story-telling.

Life changing awesomeness.
Brene's research is changing my life.

She has given me a new vocabulary for things I knew needed words but couldn't understand.

24
DEEP WORK
AUTHOR: CAL NEWPORT

Rules for Focused Success in a Distracted World

Amazon (US) star rating: 4.6 ★

Number of Amazon (US) reviews: 4,620

Published: 2016

About the author:

Cal Newport, Ph.D. is a computer science professor at Georgetown University.

He also runs the popular website Study Hacks: Decoding Patterns of Success.

Deep Work is his fifth book.

He lives in an old Victorian house in Maryland with his wife and children.

www.calnewport.com

more about
DEEP WORK

- Deep work is the ability to focus without distraction on a cognitively demanding task. It's a skill that allows you to quickly master complicated information and produce better results in less time.
- Deep work will make you better at what you do and provide the sense of true fulfillment that comes from craftsmanship.
- In short, deep work is like a super power in our increasingly competitive twenty-first century economy.
- And yet, most people have lost the ability to go deep-spending their days instead in a frantic blur of e-mail and social media, not even realizing there's a better way.
- In DEEP WORK, author and professor Cal Newport flips the narrative on impact in a connected age.
- Instead of arguing distraction is bad, he instead celebrates the power of its opposite.
- Dividing this book into two parts, he first makes the case that in almost any profession, cultivating a deep work ethic will produce massive benefits. He then presents a rigorous training regimen, presented as a series of four "rules," for transforming your mind and habits to support this skill.

WHAT OTHERS SAY:

"Cal Newport is a clear voice in a sea of noise, bringing science and passion in equal measure. We don't need more clicks, more cats, and more emojis. We need brave work, work that happens when we refuse to avert our eyes."—Seth Godin

I have read a lot of books on personal development and self help, most of them useless. This however is a true gem. I put it in the top 5 most useful books I have ever read.

25
THE DESIRE MAP
AUTHOR: DANIELLE LAPORTE
A Guide to Creating Goals with Soul

Amazon star rating: 4.5 ★

Number of Amazon reviews: 625

Published: 2014

Danielle LaPorte was a bartender, an apartment manager, a nanny, and eventually... she ran her own publicity agency, and a future-studies think tank studying trends for the likes of the Pentagon and the World Bank.

Now, she writes poetry and speaks about conscious living.

She's also a mother to a teenage son.

Named one of the "Top 100 Websites for Women" by Forbes, over 5 million people a month visit DanielleLaPorte.com for her regular #Truthbombs and poetry, and what's been called "the best place online for kickass spirituality."

Marianne Williamson refers to Danielle "as a bright light in the modern priestesshood." Eve Ensler calls her "a force field of energy, wonder, humour, and love."

Danielle's charities of choice are VDay: a global activist movement to end violence against women and girls; and charity: water, setting out to bring safe drinking water to everyone in the world.

She lives in Vancouver, Canada.

daniellelaporte.com IG *@daniellelaporte*

more about
THE DESIRE MAP

- Your bucket list. Quarterly objectives. Strategic plans. Lots of goals and plans to achieve those goals—no matter what. Except ...
- You're not chasing the goal itself, you're actually chasing the feeling that you hope achieving that goal will give you.
- Which is the procedures of achievement upside down.
- We go after the stuff we want to have, get, or accomplish, and we hope that we'll be fulfilled when we get there.
- It's backwards. And it's burning us out.
- So what if you first got clear on how you actually wanted to feel in your life, and then created some "Goals with Soul"?
- Danielle brings you a holistic life-planning tool that will revolutionize the way you go after what you want in life.
- Unapologetically passionate and with plenty of warm wit, LaPorte turns the concept of ambition inside out and offers an inspired, refreshingly practical workbook for using the Desire Map process:
  1. Identify your "core desired feelings" in every life domain: livelihood & lifestyle, body & wellness, creativity & learning, relationships & society, and essence & spirituality
  2. Create practical "Goals with Soul" to generate your core desired feelings
  3. Why easing up on your expectations actually liberates you to reach your goals
  4. Self-assessment quizzes, worksheets, and complete Desire Mapping tools for creating the life you truly long for
- Goal-setting just got a makeover.

WHAT OTHERS SAY:

This is a must read for anyone with a dream. Out of all of the self-help books, I have read recently The Desire Map lifted my spirits.

How empowering. I read the book to gain some clarity and because I love going in depth when navigating hard choices and decision making. Scary, at times. Unsettling, at times. So much worth it.

26
DISRUPT-HER
AUTHOR: MIKI AGRAWAL

A Manifesto for the Modern Woman. A Rallying Cry for Women to Radically Question the Status Quo.

Amazon (US) star rating: 4.5 ★
Number of Amazon (US) reviews: 103 (newcomer)
Published: 2020

About the author:

Miki Agrawal is a serial social entrepreneur.
She was the recipient of The Tribeca Film Festival's Disruptive Innovation Award, she was named 2017 Young Global Leader by the World Economic Forum and Social Entrepreneur of the Year by the World Technology Summit, she was one of INC magazine's Most Impressive Women Entrepreneurs of 2016 etc.
She is the founder of the acclaimed farm-to-table alternative pizza concept called WILD.
She co-founded and built THINX, a high-tech, period-proof underwear brand. She most recently founded TUSHY (www.hellotushy.com), a company that is revolutionizing the American toilet category.
Miki is an identical twin, half-Japanese, half-Indian French Canadian, former professional soccer player, graduate of Cornell University, and proud mama of Hiro Happy.

www.mikiagrawal.com   IG: @mikiagrawal

more about DISRUPT-HER

- In order to navigate the complicated--at times maddening - struggles of contemporary femininity, we need an unabashed manifesto for the modern woman that inspires us to move past outrage and take positive steps on the personal, professional, and societal levels.
- This manifesto galvanizes us to action in 13 major areas of our lives with as much fire power as possible.
- These are the credos we live by, the advice we give to friends, the tenets we instill in our companies and peers on a daily basis.
- Stories of badass female movers and shakers are shared in this book too to give you an extra jolt of "I've got this."
- It's a whole body F*CK YES to your work, your love, your relationships, and your mission-while doing it all authentically, unapologetically, and with full integrity.

WHAT OTHERS SAY:

Amazing book. Gets right to the heart of what keeps most people bound, contained, and unhappy.
Miki's voice is raw and straight up, no punches pulled. It's exactly what's needed if you're ready to show up fully.

"Disrupt-Her is a book that will upgrade your mental conditioning and help you rethink your life from top to bottom." – Jim Kwik, celebrity brain coach and founder, Kwik Learning

27
DO LESS
AUTHOR: KATE NORTHRUP

A Revolutionary Approach to Time and Energy Management for Busy Moms

Amazon (US) star rating: 4.5 ★
Number of Amazon (US) reviews: 210
Published: 2019

About the author:

As an entrepreneur, bestselling author, podcaster, speaker, and mother, Kate Northrup has built a multimedia educational platform that reaches hundreds of thousands globally.

She's committed to supporting ambitious women to light up the world without burning themselves out.

Kate teaches data and soul-driven time and energy management practices that result in saving time, making more money, and experiencing less stress through her Do Less Planner, her programs, and her books, Do Less and Money: A Love Story.

Kate's work has been featured by The Today Show, The New York Times, Harvard Business Review, Yahoo! Finance, Forbes, Women's Health, Glamour, and more.

Kate lives with her husband their daughters in a cozy town in Maine.
katenorthrup.com   IG: *@katenorthrup*

more about
DO LESS

- This is a book for working women and mothers who are ready to release the culturally inherited belief that their worth is equal to their productivity, and instead create a personal and professional life that's based on presence, meaning, and joy.
- As opposed to focusing on "fitting it all in", time management, and leaning in, as so many books geared at ambitious women do, this book embraces the notion that through doing less women can have - and be - more.
- The addiction to busyness and the obsession with always trying to do more leads women, especially working mothers, to feel like they're always failing their families, their careers, their spouses, and themselves.
- This book will give women the permission and tools to change the way they approach their lives and allow them to embrace living in tune with the cyclical nature of the feminine, cutting out the extraneous busyness from their lives so they have more satisfaction and joy, and letting themselves be more often instead of doing all the time.
- Do Less offers the listener a series of 14 experiments to try to see what would happen if she did less in one specific way.
- So, rather than approaching doing less as an entire life overhaul (which is overwhelming in and of itself), this book gives the listener bite-sized steps to try incorporating over two weeks!

WHAT OTHERS SAY:

I lOVE this book. It is revolutionary.
Imagine a time management system that relaxes your body and soul and mind and in so doing makes you more effective! I have been practicing Kate's Do Less system from her online material and it has transformed my life, my sleep and settled my nervous system.

Five stars. Full of easy "experiments" that make a huge difference.

28
DON'T KEEP YOUR DAY JOB

AUTHOR: CATHY HELLER

How to Turn Your Passion into Your Career

Amazon (US) star rating: 4.5 ★

Number of Amazon (US) reviews: 269

Published: 2019

About the author:

As the creator and host of Don't Keep Your Day Job, Cathy Heller is growing one of the biggest, most engaged audiences in podcasting. DKYDJ averages 180,000 listeners around the world weekly and has over 2,300 5-star reviews on Apple Podcasts and was nominated for a Webby Award for Best Business Podcast.

Prior to her podcast, Cathy handcrafted a career as a songwriter, licensing her music to film/TV and advertising.

She loves Swedish fish, autumn leaves and Broadway shows.

When she's not hosting the podcast, coaching, speaking or songwriting, she is singing along to Frozen with her three girls and making buttered pasta.

cathyheller.com   *IG @cathy.heller*

more about
DON'T KEEP YOUR DAY JOB

- The pursuit of happiness is all about finding our purpose.
- We don't want to just go to work and build someone else's dream, we want to do our life's work.
- But how do we find out what we're supposed to contribute?
- What are those key ingredients that push those who succeed to launch their ideas high into the sky, while the rest of us remain stuck on the ground?
- Don't Keep Your Day Job will get you fired up, ready to rip it open and use your zone of genius to add a little more sparkle to this world.
- Cathy Heller shares wisdom, anecdotes, and practical suggestions from successful creative entrepreneurs and experts, including actress Jenna Fischer on rejection, Gretchen Rubin on the keys to happiness, Jen Sincero on having your best badass life, and so much more.
- You'll learn essential steps like how to build your side hustle, how to find your tribe, how to reach for what you truly deserve, and how to ultimately turn your passion into profit and build a life you love.

WHAT OTHERS SAY:

"Cathy really 'gets it.' Listen to Don't Keep Your Day Job! It is filled with the advice people need to pursue their passions and make their lives more meaningful." —Emily Giffin, #1 bestselling novelist

Fleshing out an idea, or wondering how to take yours to the next level, do yourself a favor and buy this book. I've ordered several for my daughter and her friends as they move into the side hustle economy. Next, subscribe to her Don't Keep Your Day Job podcast for a twice a week blast of enthusiasm and encouragement.

29
DOTCOM SECRETS

AUTHOR: RUSSELL BRUNSON

The Underground Playbook for Growing Your Company Online with Sales Funnels

Amazon (US) star rating: 4.5 ★

Number of Amazon (US) reviews: 1,631

Published: 2015

About the author:

Russell Brunson is a serial entrepreneur who started his first online company while he was wrestling at Boise State University.

Within a year of graduating he had sold over a million dollars worth of his own products and services from his basement!

For over 10 years now Russell has been starting and scaling companies online.

Russell has built a following of over a million entrepreneurs, sold hundreds of thousands of copies of his best selling books, popularized the concept of sales funnels, and co-founded a software company called ClickFunnelsthat helps tens of thousands of entrepreneurs quickly get their message out to the marketplace.

russellbrunson.com

more about
DOTCOM SECRETS

- DotCom Secrets is not just another "how-to" book on internet marketing.
- This book is not about getting more traffic to your website--yet these secrets will help you get exponentially more traffic than ever before.
- Low traffic or low conversion rates are symptoms of a much greater problem that's a little harder to see (that's the bad news), but a lot easier to fix (that's the good news).
- What most businesses really have is a "funnel" problem. Your funnel is the online process that you take your potential customers through to turn them into actual customers.
- Everyone has a funnel (even if they don't realize it), and yours is either bringing more customers to you or repelling them.
- Over the past decade we have run tens of thousands of split tests to figure out which funnels work for almost every situation you can dream of. If your goal is to generate leads, we have funnel frameworks and scripts for that. If you want to sell a product or a service, there are frameworks and scripts for that as well.
- The sales funnel frameworks that you will find inside these pages have now helped literally tens of thousands of companies around the world to grow faster than ever before.
- This book will give you access to all the processes, funnels, frameworks, and scripts that we use to scale our companies online so you can fix your funnel and turn it into the most profitable member of your team!

WHAT OTHERS SAY

"I've underlined something on almost every page!
I wish I wrote this book -it's really that good!"
Jeff Walker, #1 NY Times bestselling author of Launch

When someone has so gifted has gone through all the pain in their career and then writes about the solutions, not to follow their lead if you are into online selling is a recipe for disaster.

30
EAT THAT FROG

AUTHOR: BRIAN TRACY

21 Great Ways to Stop Procrastinating and Get More Done in Less Time

Amazon (US) star rating: 4.7 ★
Number of Amazon (US) reviews: 2,667
Published: 2017

About the author:

Brian Tracy is chairman and CEO of Brian Tracy International.

As a keynote speaker and seminar leader, he addresses more than 250,000 people each year.

He is the bestselling author of more than eighty books that have been translated into dozens of languages.

He has served as a consultant and trainer to more than 1,000 corporations and more than 10,000 medium-sized enterprises in more than seventy-five countries.

briantracy.com

more about
EAT THAT FROG

- There's an old saying that if the first thing you do each morning is eat a live frog, you'll have the satisfaction of knowing you're done with the worst thing you'll have to do all day.
- For Tracy, eating a frog is a metaphor for tackling your most challenging task—but also the one that can have the greatest positive impact on your life.
- Eat That Frog! shows you how to organize each day so you can zero in on these critical tasks and accomplish them efficiently and effectively.
- The core of what is vital to effective time management is: decision, discipline, and determination.
- And in this fully revised and updated edition, Tracy adds two new chapters.
- The first explains how you can use technology to remind yourself of what is most important and protect yourself from what is least important.
- The second offers advice for maintaining focus in our era of constant distractions, electronic and otherwise.
- This life-changing book will ensure that you get more of your important tasks done today.

WHAT OTHERS SAY
"This book gave me the kick in the pants I needed to organize my to do lists, plan my days, become more productive, and get focused."

A Must Read for Procrastinators I'm the king of procrastination, and I needed this book to help me get out of my rut.

31
THE E-MYTH (REVISITED)
AUTHOR: MICHAEL E. GERBER

Why Most Small Businesses Don't Work and What to Do About It

Amazon (US) star rating: 4.7 ★

Number of Amazon (US) reviews: 4,140

Published: 2004

About the author:

Michael E. Gerber is a true legend of entrepreneurship.

The editors of INC magazine called him "The World's #1 Small Business Guru."

He is Co-founder and Chairman of the Michael E. Gerber Companies —a group of highly unique enterprises dedicated to creating world-class start-ups and entrepreneurs in every industry and economy.

The Gerber Companies transforms the way small business owners grow their enterprises and has evolved into an empire over its history of nearly three decades.

michaelegerbercompanies.com

more about
THE E-MYTH (REVISITED)

- E-Myth \ 'e-,'mith\ n 1: the entrepreneurial myth: the myth that most people who start small businesses are entrepreneurs 2: the fatal assumption that an individual who understands the technical work of a business can successfully run a business that does that technical work
- Voted #1 business book by Inc. 500 CEOs.
- An instant classic, this revised and updated edition of the phenomenal bestseller dispels the myths about starting your own business.
- Small business consultant and author Michael E. Gerber, with sharp insight gained from years of experience, points out how common assumptions, expectations, and even technical expertise can get in the way of running a successful business.
- Gerber walks you through the steps in the life of a business—from entrepreneurial infancy through adolescent growing pains to the mature entrepreneurial perspective: the guiding light of all businesses that succeed—and shows how to apply the lessons of franchising to any business, whether or not it is a franchise. Most importantly, Gerber draws the vital, often overlooked distinction between working on your business and working in your business.

WHAT OTHERS SAY:
"Thanks to Gerber I have freed up over three hours a day, significantly increased my sales, more than doubled my bottom line, and been able to take my first vacation in four years."

This book literally changed my life. II had been struggling for years doing all managerial work myself so that it was done up to my standards. We did great work but at the expense of my sanity!
The E-Myth was the driving factor that took my small business which had been controlling my life and transformed it into a business I could run remotely.

32
THE ENTREPRENEUR MIND
AUTHOR: KEVIN D. JOHNSON

100 Essential Beliefs, Characteristics, and Habits of Elite Entrepreneurs

Amazon (US) star rating: 4.6 ★

Number of Amazon (US) reviews: 574

Published: 2013

About the author:
Kevin D. Johnson, president of Johnson Media Inc. and a serial entrepreneur, has several years of experience leading his multimillion-dollar marketing and communications company that now serves many of the most notable global businesses, such as Porsche, Chase, and The Coca-Cola Company.

As an innovative leader, he has appeared on CNN, ABC's Good Morning America, CBS, and in The New York Times and The Wall Street Journal.

In his spare time, Kevin enjoys lecturing around the world, serving on boards, volunteering for nonprofits, listening to salsa and jazz, playing piano in his Latin band, reading, golfing, traveling, and running marathons.

johnsonmedia.com

more about
THE ENTREPRENEUR MIND

- To achieve unimaginable business success and financial wealth—to reach the upper echelons of entrepreneurs, where you'll find Mark Zuckerberg of Facebook, Sara Blakely of Spanx, Mark Pincus of Zynga, Kevin Plank of Under Armour, and many others—you have to change the way you think.
- In other words, you must develop the Entrepreneur Mind, a way of thinking that comes from learning the vital lessons of the best entrepreneurs.
- Through the conviction of his own personal experiences, which include a life-changing visit to Harvard Business School, and the compelling stories of modern-day business tycoons, Johnson transforms a complex topic into a lucid and accessible one.
- In this riveting book written for new and veteran entrepreneurs, Johnson identifies one hundred key lessons that every entrepreneur must learn in seven areas: Strategy, Education, People, Finance, Marketing and Sales, Leadership, and Motivation.

WHAT OTHERS SAY:
"Kevin stitches together actual life scenarios and outcomes that every entrepreneur needs to understand.
This book doesn't live in the clouds like some others do.
Real life for real business builders... read it!"

There are many themes in this book that spoke to me, however an over-arching concept that occurred throughout, is one discussed in section #43 "You are odd and it's ok".
This is an essential mentality for anyone in the startup world.

33
ESSENTIALISM
AUTHOR: GREG MCKEOWN

The Disciplined Pursuit of Less

Amazon (US) star rating: 4.6 ★
Number of Amazon (US) reviews: 4,072
Published: 2014

About the author:

Greg McKeown writes, teaches, and speaks around the world on the importance of living and leading as an Essentialist.
He has spoken at companies including Apple, Google, Facebook, LinkedIn, Salesforce, Symantec, and Twitter and is among the most popular bloggers for the Harvard Business Review and LinkedIn Influencer's group.
He co-created the course, Designing Life, Essentially at Stanford University, was a collaborator of the Wall Street Journal bestseller Multipliers and serves as a Young Global Leader for the World Economic Forum.
He holds an MBA from Stanford University.
Originally from London, England, McKeown now lives in Calabasas, California with his wife, Anna, and their four children.

gregmckeown.com   IG @gregorymckeown

more about
ESSENTIALISM

- Essentialism isn't about getting more done in less time. It's about getting only the right things done.
- Have you ever:
- found yourself stretched too thin?
- simultaneously felt overworked and under-utilised?
- felt busy but not productive?
- felt like your time is constantly hijacked by others' agendas?
- If you answered yes to any of these, the way out is the Way of the Essentialist.
- Essentialism is more than a time-management strategy or a productivity technique.
- It is a systematic discipline for discerning what is absolutely essential, then eliminating everything that is not, so we can make the highest possible contribution toward the things that really matter.
- By forcing us to apply more selective criteria for what is Essential, the disciplined pursuit of less empowers us to reclaim control of our own choices about where to spend our precious time and energy—instead of giving others the implicit permission to choose for us.
- Essentialism is not one more thing—it's a whole new way of doing everything. It's about doing less, but better, in every area of our lives. It's is a movement whose time has come.

WHAT OTHERS SAY:
"A timely, essential read for anyone who feels overcommitted, overloaded, or overworked."–Adam Grant

I read this 1-2 times a year. This has become my go-to book whenever I feel overwhelmed with life.

34
EVERYTHING IS FIGUREOUTABLE

AUTHOR: MARIE FORLEO

Whether you want to leave a dead end job, break an addiction, learn to dance, heal a relationship, or grow a business, Everything is Figureoutable will show you how.

Amazon (US) star rating: 4.8 ★
Number of Amazon (US) reviews: 2,405
Published: 2019

About the author:
A born-and-raised Jersey girl with nothing more than passion, a laptop and a dream, Marie Forleo has created a socially conscious digital empire that inspires millions across the globe.
Named by Oprah as a thought leader for the next generation, she's the star of the award-winning show MarieTV, with over 50 million views, and host of The Marie Forleo Podcast, with more than ten million downloads.
Marie has taught entrepreneurs, artists, and multipassionate go-getters from all walks of life how to dream big and back it up with daily action to create results.
She runs the acclaimed business training program, B-School.

www.MarieForleo.com   IG: @marieforleo

more about
EVERYTHING IS FIGUREOUTABLE

- It's more than just a fun phrase to say. It's a philosophy of relentless optimism. A mindset. A mantra. A conviction.
- While most self-help books offer quick fixes, Everything is Figureoutable will retrain your brain to think more creatively and positively in the face of setbacks.
- In the words of Cheryl Strayed, it's "a must-read for anyone who wants to face their fears, fulfill their dreams, and find a better way forward."
- If you're having trouble solving a problem or reaching a dream, the problem isn't you. It's that you haven't yet installed the one belief that changes everything.
- Marie's mom once told her, "Nothing in life is that complicated. You can do whatever you set your mind to if you roll up your sleeves. Everything is figureoutable."
- You'll learn:
  -The habit that makes it 42% more likely you'll achieve your goals.
  -How to overcome a lack of time and money.
  -How to deal with criticism and imposter syndrome.

WHAT OTHERS SAY:

"Everything is Figureoutable is a whirlwind of power, humor, pragmatism, and grace. Marie Forleo writes exactly the way she lives— with full-on enthusiasm, no-bullshit directness, and a ferocious commitment to self-accountability. This woman is the real deal, people. This book will change lives."
-Elizabeth Gilbert, author of Eat, Pray, Love and Big Magic

I am loving this book so much!!! Not yet finished and never want it to end. I have had so many shifts in my mindset from reading this. Loads of little nuggets of gold that would be worth the price of the book for even one of those insights and there are tons. Everyone should read it!

35
EXPERT SECRETS
AUTHOR: RUSSELL BRUNSON

The Underground Playbook for Creating a Mass Movement of People Who Will Pay for Your Advice

Amazon (US) star rating: 4.5 ★
Number of Amazon (US) reviews: 685
Published: 2017

About the author:
Russell Brunson is a serial entrepreneur who started his first online company while he was wrestling at Boise State University.

Within a year of graduating he had sold over a million dollars worth of his own products and services from his basement!

For over 10 years now Russell has been starting and scaling companies online.

Russell has built a following of over a million entrepreneurs, sold hundreds of thousands of copies of his best selling books, popularized the concept of sales funnels, and co-founded a software company called ClickFunnelsthat helps tens of thousands of entrepreneurs quickly get their message out to the marketplace.

russellbrunson.com

more about
EXPERT SECRETS

- It doesn't matter what message, product, or service you are selling online, if you don't build a mass movement of people who will pay to hear your message, it's unlikely you will achieve success.
- Expert Secrets Will Help You Too
- Find your voice and give you the confidence to become a leader
- Build a mass movement of people whose lives you can affect...
- Make this calling a career, where people will pay you for your advice.
- Your message has the ability to change someone's life.
- The impact that the right message can have on someone at the right time in their life is immeasurable.
- It could help to save marriages, repair families, change someone's health, grow a company or more...
- But only if you know how to get it into the hands of the people whose lives you have been called to change.
- Expert Secrets will show you how.

WHAT OTHERS SAY:

Best book ever for marketing your business. And not just for online marketing. This book goes into so much detail and is perfect for any business. How to tell stories to make sales.
How to be the EXPERT in your Niche.

I lost $$thousands more running ads trying to figure out what I was missing... until I came across this book.

Read it, then read it again. A great read for any entrepreneur! I found myself being challenged to think throughout the entire book.

36
FEAR IS NOT THE BOSS OF YOU

AUTHOR: JENNIFER ALLWOOD

How to Get Out of Your Head and Live the Life You Were Made For

Amazon (US) star rating: 4.8 ★
Number of Amazon (US) reviews: 1,206
Published: 2020

About the author:
What started as a desire to help pull her family out of financial desperation became a calling to help other women find the courage to do the same.

Today Jennifer is able to use her social media following of 500K people, her podcast, The Jennifer Allwood Show, with more than 1.5m downloads, her coaching groups with thousands of members, and this book to help other women do for their businesses what she has done in hers.

Jennifer Allwood is a passionate cheerleader of women who adds biblical truth to the modern day "dream big" mantra. Her no-nonsense approach to doing things you are scared to do and saying yes to God is helping women everywhere build the life and business of their dreams. She's lives n Kansas City with Mr. Magic (her husband, Jason) and their four wild kiddos—Noah, Easton, Ava Grace, and their new bonus kiddo, Ariana. Oh, and their Goldendoodles, Stella and Lola, the best dogs on earth.

jenniferallwood.com   IG @jenniferallwood

more about
FEAR IS NOT THE BOSS OF YOU

- Your future and your destiny is too important.
- Discover how to get unstuck and over your fear
- This book is for any woman who has ever been overwhelmed with indecision, paralyzed with fear, or just plain stuck. With no-nonsense biblical truth, Fear Is Not the Boss of You is a loving kick in the backside that will catapult you into ACTION.
- Successful entrepreneur, business coach, and girl next door Jennifer Allwood is your guide to show you why you can't stay stuck, teaching you how to get out of your own way and get on the road to fulfilling the life of your dreams--even if you're afraid.
- Whether you're thinking of launching a new business, adopting a child, writing a book, or competing in a triathlon, Jennifer will motivate you to move from paralyzing fear into courageous obedience and action. Jennifer will show you how to:
1. Identify how and where you are stuck
2. Determine what's holding you back
3. Get out of your own way
4. Empower those around you
5. Experience the incredible joy that comes from trusting a big God to do big things in you and through you
- This is your gutsy invitation to go after the big dream God has called you to . . . because fear is not the boss of you.

WHAT OTHERS SAY:
A crucial message that I needed to hear as I was starting a new business at 56 years old and was just the loving, truth-filled, kick in the butt I needed!
Jennifer has a way of making you feel like you are sharing a table at lunch for girlfriend time with the friend that you trust to speak the real truth to you - even when she knows it may sting a little.

I have read countless books in the past few years on self growth and development, business building or spiritual development.
NEVER have I read one that had all three in one book.

37
THE 5AM CLUB
AUTHOR: ROBIN SHARMA

Own Your Morning.
Elevate Your Life.

Amazon (US) star rating: 4. 5 ★
Number of Amazon (US) reviews: 6,248
Published: 2018

About the author:

A former lawyer, Robin Sharma quit his job and self-published a
book at a Kinko's copy shop (his mother edited it). He stored 2,000
copies in his kitchen.
His second book The Monk Who Sold His Ferrari was also originally
self-published until former HarperCollins president Ed Carson
discovered Robin in a bookstore.
The book, and the series that followed, have become one of the
world's most successful publishing franchises.
He is a globally respected humanitarian.
Widely considered one of the world's top leadership and personal
optimization advisors, his clients include famed billionaires,
professional sports superstars and many Fortune 100 companies.
The author's #1 bestsellers such as The Monk Who Sold His Ferrari,
The Greatness Guide and The Leader Who Had No Title, are in over
92 languages making him one of the most broadly read writers alive
today.

www.robinsharma.com   IG @robinsharma

more about
THE 5AM CLUB

- Part manifesto for mastery, part playbook for genius-grade productivity and part companion for a life lived beautifully, The 5am Club is a work that will transform your life. Forever.
- Through this book, researched over a rigorous four-year period, you will discover the early-rising habit that has helped so many accomplish epic results while upgrading their happiness, helpfulness and feelings of aliveness.
- Through an enchanting—and often amusing—story about two struggling strangers who meet an eccentric tycoon who becomes their secret mentor, The 5am Club will walk you through:
- How great geniuses, business titans and the world's wisest people start their mornings to produce astonishing achievements
- A little-known formula you can use instantly to wake up early feeling inspired, focused and flooded with a fiery drive to get the most out of each day
- A step-by-step method to protect the quietest hours of daybreak so you have time for exercise, self-renewal and personal growth
- A neuroscience-based practice proven to help make it easy to rise while most people are sleeping, giving you precious time for yourself to think, express your creativity and begin the day peacefully instead of being rushed
- "Insider-only" tactics to defend your gifts, talents and dreams against digital distraction and trivial diversions so you enjoy fortune, influence and a magnificent impact on the world

WHAT OTHERS SAY:
I would give it 10 stars if I could.
A true masterpiece. This is quite possibly the best book I have read and I am an avid book reader.

This book transformed my life. It's not just rising at 5am. It's what you do throughout your day to build world class.

38
THE 5 SECOND RULE
AUTHOR: MEL ROBINS

Transform your Life, Work, and Confidence with Everyday Courage

Amazon (US) star rating: 4.5 ★
Number of Amazon (US) reviews: 3,383
Published: 2017

About the author:
In her own words: At age 41, I life was a mess. I was unemployed. Facing bankruptcy. Marriage spiraling. Confidence shot. Hitting the bottle hard.

Now she is the most booked female speaker in the world and an international best-selling author whose work has been translated into 36 languages. 2017, Mel broke self- publishing records with her international best-seller The 5 Second Rule.
It was named the #1 audiobook in the world and the fifth most read book of the year on Amazon.
When Mel launched her science backed productivity planner, The 5 Second Journal, the first print run sold out worldwide within minutes.

Her TEDx Talk is one of the most popular of all time, with more than 18 million views.
melrobbins.com   IG: @melrobbins

more about
THE 5 SECOND RULE

- How to enrich your life and destroy doubt in five seconds.
- Throughout your life, you've had parents, coaches, teachers, friends, and mentors who have pushed you to be better than your excuses and bigger than your fears.
- What if the secret to having the confidence and courage to enrich your life and work is simply knowing how to push yourself?
- Using the science of habits, riveting stories, and surprising facts from some of the most famous moments in history, art, and business, Mel Robbins will explain the power of a "push moment". Then, she'll give you one simple tool you can use to become your greatest self.
- It takes just five seconds to use this tool, and every time you do you'll be in great company.
- More than eight million people have watched Mel's TEDx Talk, and executives inside of the world's largest brands are using the tool to increase productivity, collaboration, and engagement.
- The 5 Second Rule is a simple, one-size-fits-all solution for the one problem we all face - we hold ourselves back. The secret isn't knowing what to do,it's knowing how to make yourself do it.

WHAT OTHERS SAY:

Mel Robbins has over 11 million views on Youtube for her Ted talk, "How To Stop Screwing Yourself Over." When you read this book, you'll understand why. The 5 Second Rule helps you build an excellent habit that will transform your life.

Simple and powerful advice. It's not possible to find a quicker way to change your behavior in so big form. It's simple to do the right thing, and use the countdown from 5 to 1 and then Go.
In the book, Mel do a series of examples for different situations, from getting out of bed on time -my main use- to overcome the panic to flight, by example. Very useful book. It changed my life.

39
THE 4-HOUR WORKWEEK

AUTHOR: TIM FERRIS

Escape the 9-5, Live Anywhere and Join the New Rich

Amazon (US) star rating: 4.5 ★
Number of Amazon (US) reviews: 8,840
Published: 2011

About the author:
TIMOTHY FERRISS is a serial entrepreneur, #1 New York Times bestselling author, and angel investor/advisor (Facebook, Twitter, Evernote, Uber, and 20+ more).
Best known for his rapid-learning techniques, Tim's books -- The 4-Hour Workweek, The 4-Hour Body, and The 4-Hour Chef -- have been published in 30+ languages.
The 4-Hour Workweek has spent seven years on The New York Times bestseller list.
Tim has been featured by more than 100 media outlets including The New York Times, The Economist, TIME, Forbes, Fortune, Outside, NBC, CBS, ABC, Fox and CNN.
He has guest lectured in entrepreneurship at Princeton University since 2003. His popular blog www has 1M+ monthly readers, and his Twitter account @tferriss was selected by Mashable as one of only five "Must-Follow" accounts for entrepreneurs.
Tim's primetime TV show, The Tim Ferriss Experiment (www.upwave.com/tfx), teaches rapid-learning techniques for helping viewers to produce seemingly superhuman results in minimum time.

fourhourblog.com   IG @timferriss

more about
THE 4-HOUR WORKWEEK

- Forget the old concept of retirement and the rest of the deferred-life plan–there is no need to wait and every reason not to, especially in unpredictable economic times.
- Whether your dream is escaping the rat race, experiencing high-end world travel, or earning a monthly five-figure income with zero management, The 4-Hour Workweek is the blueprint.
- This step-by-step guide to luxury lifestyle design teaches:

1. How Tim went from $40,000 per year and 80 hours per week to $40,000 per month and 4 hours per week
2. How to outsource your life to overseas virtual assistants for $5 per hour and do whatever you want
3. How blue-chip escape artists travel the world without quitting their jobs
4. How to eliminate 50% of your work in 48 hours using the principles of a forgotten Italian economist
5. How to trade a long-haul career for short work bursts and frequent "mini-retirements"

The new expanded edition includes:

• More than 50 practical tips and case studies from readers (including families) who have doubled income, overcome common sticking points, and reinvented themselves using the original book as a starting point
• Real-world templates you can copy for eliminating e-mail, negotiating with bosses and clients, or getting a private chef for less than $8 a meal
• The latest tools and tricks, as well as high-tech shortcuts, for living like a diplomat or millionaire without being either

WHAT OTHERS SAY:

"Stunning and amazing. From mini-retirements to outsourcing your life, it's all here. Whether you're a wage slave or a Fortune 500 CEO, this book will change your life!" Phil Town, #1 NYT Bestselling Author

The 4-Hour Workweek is a new way of solving a very old problem: just how can we work to live and prevent our lives from being all about work? A world of infinite options awaits those who would read this book and be inspired by it!" Michael E. Gerber, E-Myth Worldwide

40
GET OVER YOUR DAMN SELF
AUTHOR: ROMI NEUSTADT

The No-BS Blueprint to Building a Life-Changing Business

Amazon (US) star rating: 4.7 ★
Number of Amazon (US) reviews: 1,856
Published: 2016

About the author:
Romi Neustadt is a former corporate chick (first a lawyer, then a PR executive) who traded in the billable hour to become an entrepreneur, a business coach and a speaker.

She built a 7-figure business in less than three years and wrote this book to help others maximize the potential of the direct sales channel. It was awarded a GOLD AWARD from the Nonfiction Authors Association. Her second book, You Can Have It All, Just Not at the Same Damn Time, her no-BS blueprint to living the life you really want, was published in 2020 by Portfolio | Penguin Random House.
Romi has been featured in Forbes, Inc., Fast Company and Success, and has appeared on morning shows around the country. Romi lives in San Diego with her husband John and their two kids, Nate and Bebe.

To learn more about Romi and her work, visit **romineustadt.com**

more about
GET OVER YOUR DAMN SELF

- Romi Neustadt is passionate about helping others build lucrative direct sales and network marketing businesses that help create lives with more freedom and flexibility, greater purpose and a lot more fun.
- In this book she offers you the same direct, no-BS coaching she's given to tens of thousands to help you acquire the skills to build this sucker and teach your team to do the same.
- And, equally important, she'll work on your mindset so you stop over complicating it all and stop letting the negative voices in your head win.
- You're going to learn:* The Posture to confidently connect with anyone about your business and your products.* The Possibilities for a lucrative, efficient and enormously rewarding turn key business.* The Power that's already within you to build the life you really want...if you dare.

WHAT OTHERS SAY:

#GOYDS is BRILLIANT!!!
I love Romi's no nonsense style and like me, she uses some colorful language, because let's face it, sometimes it's necessary to get your point across!!! I bought 20 copies of this book and have been gifting it all over the country because people need to hear what Romi has to say!! I even stood in line for a very long time to get my copy signed and my pic with Romi!!! If you are stuck in your networking business, Get Over Your Damn Self, and get this book!!!

Essential read for anyone in direct sales or network marketing.
As a single mom of 3 and "successful " entrepreneur, this book spoke to me on many levels and gave me a ton of ideas on how to refocus and find that fire inside again. Will re-read more than once and recommend to everyone I speak with!

41
GETTING TO YES
AUTHORS: ROGER FISHER & WILLIAM URY
Negotiating Agreement
Without Giving In

Amazon (US) star rating: 4.5 ★

Number of Amazon (US) reviews: 2,641

First published: 1981

About the authors:

Roger D. Fisher (1922-2012), a Harvard law professor whose expertise in resolving conflicts led to a role in drafting the Camp David accords between Egypt and Israel and in ending apartheid in South Africa. Over his career, Professor Fisher eagerly brought his optimistic can-do brand of problem solving to a broad array of conflicts across the globe, from the hostage crisis in Iran to the civil war in El Salvador. His emphasis was always on addressing the mutual interests of the disputing parties instead of what separated them. It did not matter to Professor Fisher whether the warring parties reached out to him or not; he would assume they needed his help. "Most of the time he was not invited. He would invite himself," His son Elliott Fisher said. "Our sense growing up was that he would read the newspaper and think, 'Oh, shoot, there is something to fix.'"

<u>William Ury</u> is an American author, academic, anthropologist, and negotiation expert. He co-founded the Harvard Program on Negotiation. Additionally, he helped found the International Negotiation Network with former President Jimmy Carter, which worked to end civil wars around the world. Ury teaches negotiation to international corporate executives and labor leaders in order to reach mutually profitable agreements with customers, suppliers, unions and joint-venture partners.

williamury.com

more about
GETTING TO YES

- Since its original publication nearly thirty years ago, Getting to Yes has helped millions of people learn a better way to negotiate.
- One of the primary business texts of the modern era, it is based on the work of the Harvard Negotiation Project, a group that deals with all levels of negotiation and conflict resolution.
- Getting to Yes offers a proven, step-by-step strategy for coming to mutually acceptable agreements in every sort of conflict.
- Thoroughly updated and revised, it offers readers a straight-forward, universally applicable method for negotiating personal and professional disputes without getting angry-or getting taken.

WHAT OTHERS SAY:
"This is by far the best thing I've ever read about negotiation."
–John Kenneth Galbraith

Getting to Yes is a highly readable, uncomplicated guide to resolving conflicts of every imaginable dimension. It teaches you how to win without compromising friendships. I wish I had written it!"
–Ann Landers

I wish I read this 20 years ago. The book has opened a world of opportunities that I could not see before. It is practical. Everyone can benefit by reading it.

42
GET VISIBLE
AUTHOR: ANNA PARKER-MAPLES
How to have more impact, influence and income

Amazon (US) star rating: 4.6 ★
Number of Amazon (US) reviews: 15
Published: 2020 (newcomer)

About the author:

Anna Parker-Naples is a multi-award-winning British entrepreneur, business coach and host of Entrepreneurs Get Visible podcast (reaching no.3 in the iTunes charts, outranking Tony Robbins, Marie Forleo, Amy Porterfield and Gary Vaynerchuk).

She lives in Bedfordshire, UK, with her husband, three children, her dog Oscar...the family cat, and two hamsters.

Anna was told in 2010 that she may never walk again due to a complication in pregnancy. Through NLP (Neuro Linguistic Programming) and mindset work, she transformed her physical health, fully recovered and embraced a journey of adventure and discovery to become the successful performer she had always dreamed she would become.

After landing herself on the red carpets in Hollywood as a celebrated Voice Actor, Anna changed focus, and now uses her skills and experience to help other entrepreneurs and creatives have the courage and strategy to become the go-to expert in their field.

She has spoked on the same platforms as celebrities such as Will Young & Ruby Wax and won an international award for her work to inspire others alongside Rio Ferdinand and singing sensation Adele. She has been featured in Metro, Psychologies, BBC Radio, iNews, Health & Wellness and Thrive Global.

Anna regularly gives keynote speeches about visibility, imposter syndrome and podcasting for authority.

www.annaparkernaples.com   IG: @annaparkernaples

more about
GET VISIBLE

- Are you wondering why you don't have the income or influence you want...yet?
- Do you want more impact within your industry, but don't know how... yet?
- Are you feeling that you're meant to do more, but don't know how to find the spotlight...yet?
- Thousands of talented, capable entrepreneurs and creatives are playing small and wondering why they aren't getting the results they deserve.
- Increasing your visibility to become the leading figure in your field isn't rocket science. It takes two things - the mindset of self-belief and a strategy for becoming an authority.
- This book takes you back to the basics of how you think about yourself and your success. The first step to becoming visible is understanding the limiting beliefs that keep you hiding and stuck.
- Once you've had those lightbulb moments, you'll learn the actions that you can take RIGHT NOW to make yourself known for what you do.

WHAT OTHERS SAY:

Insightful and practical - a helpful book for both introverts or extroverts. This book came into view just at the right time for me. Anna's story grabbed me from the start.

This book in many ways is a personal journey and that vulnerability is why it is so powerful and resonates. I challenge you to read it.

I can not recommend this book enough. Anna Parker-Naples takes you through her own journey, including the highs and lows, and how she's utilised these for her success.

This is a perfect book to help you feel inspired, motivated, and ready to become visible, influential and ready to take on the world. Be ready to go through a range of emotions as you read each chapter and fall in love with the drive & motivation behind Anna's story.

43
GET RICH LUCKY BITCH

AUTHOR: DENISE DUFFIELD-THOMAS

Release Your Money Blocks and Live a First-Class Life

Amazon (US) star rating: 4.8 ★

Number of Amazon (US) reviews: 733

Published: 2018

About the author:

Denise Duffield-Thomas is the money mindset mentor for the new wave of online female entrepreneurs.

She helps women release their fear of money, set premium prices for their services and take back control over their finances.

Her best-selling books "Lucky Bitch", "Get Rich, Lucky Bitch" and Chillpreneur give a fresh and funny road-map to create an outrageously successful life and business.

Her Money Bootcamp has helped over 6,000 students from all around the world.

In her own words, 'a lazy introvert, a Hay House author and an unbusy mother of 3'.

She owns a rose farm and lives by the beach in sunny Australia.

www.denisedt.com   www.luckybitch.com   IG: denisedt

more about
GET RICH LUCKY BITCH

- Are you ready to get rich?
- So you want to manifest more money this year. You're not alone. But why does it feel so freaking hard?
- It's weird and frankly bewildering that the most talented women in the world are often the ones struggling to make fabulous money from their talents.
- Too many female entrepreneurs sabotage their income and work too hard for too little.
- Why do most women settle for pennies instead of embracing true wealth? It's not because you're not smart or ambitious enough. You've just been programmed to block your Universal right to wealth with guilt, shame or embarrassment.
- Even if you're unaware of these blocks and fears, you're probably not earning what you're really worth.
- Are you ready to break through your money blocks and finally make the money you deserve?
- In Get Rich, Lucky Bitch! you'll learn how to unlock your hidden potential for abundance and upgrade your life forever.
- Join Denise Duffield-Thomas on a journey of self- discovery so you can smash through your abundance blocks and join a community of women all around the world who are learning to live large and become truly lucky bitches.

WHAT OTHERS SAY:

"Denise has helped her growing community of 120,000+ business owners overcome their money blocks and build successful companies."
Forbes.com

"Denise is the ultimate money mindset mentor. With her systems, tools, and tricks to open up your heart and mind to receive the abundance that is your birthright, you can't fail.
Everybody needs some Denise in their life."
Susie Moore

44
#GIRLBOSS
AUTHOR: SOPHIA AMORUSO

From dumpster diving to founding one of the fastest-growing retailers in the world.

Amazon (US) star rating: 4.6 ★
Number of Amazon (US) reviews: 2,774
Published: 2015

About the author:

Sophia Amoruso is the Founder of Nasty Gal and the Founder and CEO of Girlboss.

A creative visionary, modern-day entrepreneur, and fashion doyenne, Sophia has become one of the most prominent figures in retail and a cultural icon for a generation of women seeking ownership of their careers and futures.

Her other books are The Girlboss Workbook and Nasty Galaxy.

sophiaamoruso.com IG @sophiaamoruso

more about
#GIRLBOSS

- In the New York Times bestseller that the Washington Post called "Lean In for misfits," Sophia Amoruso shares how she went from dumpster diving to founding one of the fastest-growing retailers in the world.
- Amoruso spent her teens hitchhiking, committing petty theft, and scrounging in dumpsters for leftover bagels.
- By age twenty-two she had dropped out of school, and was broke, directionless, and checking IDs in the lobby of an art school—a job she'd taken for the health insurance.
- It was in that lobby that Sophia decided to start selling vintage clothes on eBay.
- Flash forward to today, and she's the founder of Nasty Gal and the founder and CEO of Girlboss.
- Sophia was never a typical CEO, or a typical anything, and she's written #GIRLBOSS for other girls like her: outsiders (and insiders) seeking a unique path to success, even when that path is windy as all hell and lined with naysayers.
- #GIRLBOSS proves that being successful isn't about where you went to college or how popular you were in high school.
- It's about trusting your instincts and following your gut; knowing which rules to follow and which to break; when to button up and when to let your freak flag fly.

WHAT OTHERS SAY:

"A witty and cleverly told account . . . It's this kind of honest advice, plus the humorous ups and downs of her rise in online retail, that make the book so appealing." —Los Angeles Times

"Amoruso teaches the innovative and entrepreneurial among us to play to our strengths, learn from our mistakes, and know when to break a few of the traditional rules." —Vanity Fair

"#GIRLBOSS is more than a book . . . #GIRLBOSS is a movement." —
Lena Dunham

45
GIRL CODE
AUTHOR: CARA ALWILL LEYBA

Unlocking the Secrets to Success, Sanity, and Happiness for the Female Entrepreneur

Amazon (US) star rating: 4.7 ★
Number of Amazon (US) reviews: 1,250
Published: 2017

About the author:

Cara Alwill is a New York City based creative entrepreneur who encourages women to live their most effervescent lives, celebrate themselves every day, and make their happiness a priority.

She is a best selling personal development author, mentor to women entrepreneurs, and creator of The Champagne Diet blog.
Over 7 million listeners worldwide tune in to Cara's podcast Style Your Mind each week for powerful conversations and a mega dose of inspiration.
Cara's stylish and edgy approach to personal development has attracted thousands of women to attend her workshops and events. She has been featured in Forbes, Glamour, Shape, Entrepreneur, Success, Cosmo, Marie Claire, and many others.

As a social influencer, Cara inspires her loyal following daily with lifestyle tips, mindset advice, business strategies, and does it all with a chic and fashionable flair. Cara has collaborated with Macy's, Kate Spade, SoulCycle, and others.

thechampagnediet.com IG @thechampagnediet

more about GIRL CODE

- A few years ago, I made a crazy claim in the first edition of Girl Code: that in today's competitive marketplace, the fiercest thing a female entrepreneur can do is to support other women.
- Something dynamic happens when women genuinely show up for each other. When we lose the facades, cut the bullsh*t, and truly have each other's backs.
- When we stop pretending everything is perfect, and show the messy, beautiful parts of ourselves and our work—which all look awfully similar.
- When we talk about our fears, our missteps, and our breakdowns. And most importantly, when we share our celebrations, our breakthroughs, and our solutions.
- I'm convinced that there's no reason to hoard information, connections, or insight. Wisdom is meant to be shared, so let's start sharing what we've learned to make each other better.
- Girl Code is a roadmap for female entrepreneurs, professional women, "side hustlers" (those with a day job plus a part-time small business), and anyone in between.
- This book won't teach you how to build a multimillion-dollar company. It won't teach you about systems or finance.
- But it will teach you how to build confidence in yourself, reconnect with your "why," eradicate jealousy, and ultimately learn the power of connection.
- Because at the end of the day, that's what life and business are all about.

WHAT OTHERS SAY:

This is the most riveting and inspirational women entrepreneur books I have ever read. It gave me the encouragement I need to go and make my dream a reality as a business owner.

Life changing read. An incredible book for any woman looking to make a change in their life, no matter how big or small. Cara has such an authentic and real way of writing that you feel as if you're talking to your best friend and she's giving you literally the best advice you've ever given.

46

GOOD VIBES GOOD LIFE

AUTHOR: VEX KING

How Self-Love Is the Key to Unlocking Your Greatness

Amazon (US) star rating: 4.7 ★
Number of Amazon (US) reviews: 6,818
Published: 2018

About the author:
Vex King is a social media influencer, writer, mind coach and lifestyle entrepreneur.
He experienced many challenges when he was growing up: his father died when Vex was just a baby, his family were often homeless and he grew up in troubled neighbourhoods where he regularly experienced racism.
Despite this, Vex successfully turned his whole life around. He now owns an empowering lifestyle brand, Bon Vita, which acts as a hub of positivity for anyone who wants to learn how to live a happier and more fulfilling life.
Through his popular Instagram account, Vex has become a source of inspiration for thousands of young people.
He started the Good Vibes Only #GVO movement to help others use the power of positivity to transform themselves and their lives into something greater.

vexking.com   @vexking

more about
GOOD VIBES GOOD LIFE

- Be the best version of you that YOU can be.
- How can you learn to truly love yourself? How can you transform negative emotions into positive ones? Is it possible to find lasting happiness?
- In this book, Instagram guru Vex King answers all of these questions and more.
- Vex overcame adversity to become a source of hope for thousands of young people, and now draws from his personal experience and his intuitive wisdom to inspire you to:
1. practise self-care, overcome toxic energy and prioritize your wellbeing
2. cultivate positive lifestyle habits, including mindfulness and meditation
3. change your beliefs to invite great opportunities into your life
4. manifest your goals using tried-and-tested techniques
5. overcome fear and flow with the Universe
6. find your higher purpose and become a shining light for others
- In this book, Vex will show you that when you change the way you think, feel, speak and act, you begin to change the world.

WHAT OTHERS SAY:

"Vex King is leading a revolution for the next generation of spiritual seekers. He shares deep spiritual knowledge in a way that's easy to understand, with stories from his own life, great inspirational quotes and practical solutions. Down-to-earth and relatable, this book is for anyone seeking a way out of darkness and the tools needed to build a new life they love." Soul & Spirit magazine

One of those life changing books. Through this book I read exactly what I was seeking for my future.

I COULD NOT put it down! This book is so full of live changing 'ah-ha' moments, that I ended up finishing it on Friday and am still thinking about the things I've read -and it's now Tuesday!

47
THE GREATEST YOU

AUTHOR: TRENT SHELTON

Face Reality, Release Negativity, and Live Your Purpose

Amazon (US) star rating: 4.8 ★
Number of Amazon (US) reviews: 1,881
Published: 2019

About the author:

Trent Shelton is a former NFL wide receiver who is now considered one of the most significant speakers of his generation.
He reaches over fifty million people weekly through his various social media outlets, and he travels the world speaking to people about how to create lasting change in their lives.

Trent and his wife, Maria, live in the Fort Worth, Texas, with their two children, Tristan and Maya.

trentshelton.com @trentshelton

more about
THE GREATEST YOU

- In this remarkable, life-changing new book, renowned inspirational speaker Trent Shelton shares his revolutionary tool kit for transforming your life and reaching your goals.
- Trent Shelton seemed to have it all together - until everything fell apart.
- A college football standout, his NFL dreams died when he was cut from multiple teams.
- With no job and no prospects, learning he had a child out of wedlock on the way and numbing himself with whatever he could find, Trent then found out one of his closest friends had killed himself.
- Life seemed without hope - until Trent discovered the secret to finding promise in the darkest of times. And now he shares that secret with you.
- Writing from deep, been-there experience, Trent walks you on a journey to become the best hope-filled version of yourself. In The Greatest You, Trent will help you:

1. Become everything you are meant to be
2. Face the reality of your circumstances and realize your purpose in life
3. Break free from toxic environments and forgive those who've harmed you
4. And learn how to guard yourself against the pitfalls of life

WHAT OTHERS SAY:

"If you want to become the best you, but are unsure how to get there, start here." (Rachel Hollis)

This book should be in every high school and college library.
If you are ready to take the next steps in your growth, you just found your guide. Trent Shelton time and time again hits the nail on the head. In plain relatable language.

48
GRIT

AUTHOR: ANGELA DUCKWORTH

The Power of Passion and Perseverance

Amazon (US) star rating: 4.6 ★
Number of Amazon (US) reviews: 5,115
Published: 2018

About the author:

Angela Duckworth, is the Founder and CEO of Character Lab, a nonprofit whose mission is to advance the science and practice of character development in children.
In 2013, she became a MacArthur Fellow and professor of psychology at the University of Pennsylvania.
An expert in non-I.Q. competencies, she has advised the White House, the World Bank, NBA and NFL teams, and Fortune 500 CEOs.
Prior to her career in research, she taught children math and science and was the founder of a summer school for low-income children that won the Better Government Award from the state of Massachusetts.
She completed her BA in neurobiology at Harvard, her MSc in neuroscience at Oxford, and her PhD in psychology at the University of Pennsylvania.
Angela's TED talk is among the most-viewed of all time.
Angela is also co-host, with Stephen Dubner, of the podcast No Stupid Questions.

angeladuckworth.com

more about
GRIT

- In this instant New York Times bestseller, Angela Duckworth shows anyone striving to succeed that the secret to outstanding achievement is not talent, but a special blend of passion and persistence she calls "grit."
- The daughter of a scientist who frequently noted her lack of "genius," Angela Duckworth is now a celebrated researcher and professor.
- It was her early eye-opening stints in teaching, business consulting, and neuroscience that led to her hypothesis about what really drives success: not genius, but a unique combination of passion and long-term perseverance.
- In Grit, she takes us into the field to visit cadets struggling through their first days at West Point, teachers working in some of the toughest schools, and young finalists in the National Spelling Bee.
- She also mines fascinating insights from history and shows what can be gleaned from modern experiments in peak performance.
- Finally, she shares what she's learned from interviewing dozens of high achievers—from JP Morgan CEO Jamie Dimon to New Yorker cartoon editor Bob Mankoff to Seattle Seahawks Coach Pete Carroll.

WHAT OTHERS SAY:

"Inspiration for non-geniuses everywhere"
(People)

"With Grit, Duckworth has now put out the definitive handbook for her theory of success. It parades from one essential topic to another on a float of common sense, tossing out scientific insights." —Slate

I read this on holiday and found it a real page turner. Written in an easy to read style and full of real people and real stories about success as it pertains to grittiness! It certainly hits the nail on the head - positive mental attitude plus major work ethic over simply giftedness or talent.

49
THE HAPPINESS PROJECT

AUTHOR: GRETCHEN RUBIN

Why I Spent a Year Trying to Sing in the Morning, Clean My Closets, Fight Right, Read Aristotle, and Generally Have More Fun

Amazon (US) star rating: 4.3 ★
Number of Amazon (US) reviews: 2,877
Published: 2018

About the author (in her own words):

I'm the author of THE HAPPINESS PROJECT, HAPPIER AT HOME, BETTER THAN BEFORE, THE FOUR TENDENCIES, OUTER ORDER, INNER CALM, and more.
I also have a popular, award-winning podcast, "Happier with Gretchen Rubin" (search in your favorite podcast app) and a blog (GretchenRubin.com), where I write about my daily adventures in happiness and habit-formation.
Before turning to writing, I had a career in law. A graduate of Yale and Yale Law School, I clerked for Justice Sandra Day O'Connor and was editor-in-chief of the Yale Law Journal.
I live in New York City with my husband and two daughters.

gretchenrubin.com   IG: @gretchenrubin

more about
THE HAPPINESS PROJECT

- Gretchen Rubin had an epiphany one rainy afternoon in the unlikeliest of places: a city bus. "The days are long, but the years are short," she realized. "Time is passing, and I'm not focusing enough on the things that really matter." In that moment, she decided to dedicate a year to her happiness project.
- In this lively and compelling account—now updated with new material by the author—Rubin chronicles her adventures during the twelve months she spent test-driving the wisdom of the ages, current scientific research, and lessons from popular culture about how to be happier.
- Among other things, she found that novelty and challenge are powerful sources of happiness; that money can help buy happiness, when spent wisely; that outer order contributes to inner calm; and that the very smallest of changes can make the biggest difference.
- This updated edition includes:
- An extensive new interview with the author
- Stories of other people's life-changing happiness projects
- A resource guide to the dozens of free resources created for readers
- The Happiness Project Manifesto

WHAT OTHERS SAY:

"Happiness is contagious. And so is The Happiness Project. Once you've read Gretchen Rubin's tale of a year searching for satisfaction, you'll want to start your own happiness project and get your friends and family to join you. This is the rare book that will make you both smile and think—often on the same page."
(Daniel H. Pink, author of A Whole New Mind)

"If anyone can help us stop procrastinating, start exercising or get organized, it's Gretchen Rubin. The happiness guru takes a sledgehammer to old-fashioned notions about change." (Parade)

50
HIGH PERFORMANCE HABITS

AUTHOR: BRENDON BURCHARD

How Extraordinary People Become That Way

Amazon (US) star rating: 4.7 ★

Number of Amazon (US) reviews: 2,544

Published: 2017

About the author:

Brendon Burchard is a 3-time New York Times bestselling author, a globally respected high performance coach, and one of the world's most watched, followed, and quoted personal development trainers with over 10 million followers across his brands.

O, the Oprah Magazine named him "one of the most influential leaders in personal growth."
Forbes.com named him "the world's leading high performance coach."
Larry King called him "the world's leading life coach."
Success Magazine ranks him in the Top 25 Most Influential success teachers along with Oprah Winfrey, Dr. Phil, Tony Robbins, Tim Ferriss, Arianna Huffington, and Deepak Chopra.

brendon.com   IG @brendonburchard

more about
HIGH PERFORMANCE HABITS

- After extensive original research and a decade as the world's highest-paid performance coach, Brendon Burchard finally reveals the most effective habits for reaching long-term success.
- Based on one of the largest surveys ever conducted on high performers, it turns out that just six habits move the needle the most in helping you succeed.
- Adopt these six habits and you win. Neglect them and life is a never-ending struggle.
- We all want to be high performing in every area of our lives. But how? Which habits can help you achieve long-term success and vibrant well-being no matter your age, career, strengths, or personality? To become a high performer, you must seek clarity, generate energy, raise necessity, increase productivity, develop influence, and demonstrate courage.
- This book is the art and science of how to practice these proven habits.
- If you do adopt any new habits to succeed faster, choose the habits in this book. Anyone can practice these habits, and when they do, extraordinary things happen in their lives, relationships, and careers.
- Whether you want to get more done, lead others better, develop skill faster, or dramatically increase your sense of joy and confidence, the habits in this book will help you achieve it. Each of the six habits is illustrated by cutting-edge science, thought-provoking exercises, and real-world daily practices you can implement right now.
- High Performance Habits is a science-backed, heart-centered plan to living a better quality of life.

WHAT OTHERS SAY:
Daily habits = a lifetime of results.
It's amazing the small things that you DON'T DO which make
ALL the difference to your life - good book to read if you're
trying to regulate why you're not where you could be..

51
HOW TO WIN FRIENDS AND INFLUENCE PEOPLE

AUTHOR: DALE CARNEGIE

Published in 1936. Over 30 million copies sold worldwide, making it one of the best-selling books of all time.

Amazon (US) star rating: 4.7 ★
Number of Amazon (US) reviews: 29,900
Published: 1936

About the author:

Dale Carnegie (1888-1955) described himself as a "simple country boy" from Missouri but was also a pioneer of the self-improvement genre.

Since the 1936 publication of his first book, How to Win Friends and Influence People, he has touched millions of readers and his classic works continue to impact lives to this day.

He was an American writer and lecturer, and the developer of courses in self-improvement, salesmanship, corporate training, public speaking, and interpersonal skills.

more about
HOW TO WIN FRIENDS
AND INFLUENCE PEOPLE

- You can go after the job you want—and get it
- You can take the job you have—and improve it
- You can take any situation—and make it work for you
- Dale Carnegie's rock-solid, time-tested advice has carried countless people up the ladder of success in their business and personal lives.
- One of the most groundbreaking and timeless bestsellers of all time, How to Win Friends & Influence People will teach you:
- -Six ways to make people like you
- -Twelve ways to win people to your way of thinking
- -Nine ways to change people without arousing resentment
- And much more! Achieve your maximum potential—a must-read for the twenty-first century with more than 15 million copies sold!

WHAT OTHERS SAY

My eyes have opened. I wish I had purchased this book sooner. Dale Carnegie's advice has remained constant and applicable across the years for a reason. It's simple and his techniques make perfect sense. If you're anything like me, you'll be kicking yourself when you see how you could have handled situations differently

Unlike most How to books, Carnegie is capable of bringing insight on top of telling you what to do. Imagine someone telling you to blindly follow a rule, while another makes you understand the reasoning behind his rule before giving you the choice to do it

52
THE $100 START-UP
AUTHOR: CHRIS GUILLEBEAU

Reinvent the Way You Make a Living, Do What You Love, and Create a New Future

Amazon (US) star rating: 4.5 ★

Number of Amazon (US) reviews: 2,966

Published: 2012

About the author:

During a lifetime of self-employment that included a four-year commitment as a volunteer executive in West Africa, Chris visited every country in the world (193 in total) before his 35th birthday. Since then he has modeled the proven definition of an entrepreneur: "Someone who will work 24 hours a day for themselves to avoid working one hour a day for someone else."

He is mainly interested in the convergence between highly personal goals and service to others. You can learn more about that subject in the original Brief Guide to World Domination that was read by more than 100,000 people in 60 countries during the first six months. His daily podcast, Side Hustle School, is downloaded more than 2 million times a month.

chrisguillebeau.com IG @193countries

more about
THE $100 START-UP

- Lead a life of adventure, meaning and purpose—and earn a good living.
- Still in his early thirties, Chris Guillebeau completed a tour of every country on earth and yet he's never held a "real job" or earned a regular paycheck.
- Rather, he has a special genius for turning ideas into income, and he uses what he earns both to support his life of adventure and to give back.
- Chris identified 1,500 individuals who have built businesses earning $50,000 or more from a modest investment (in many cases, $100 or less), and focused on the 50 most intriguing case studies.
- In nearly all cases, people with no special skills discovered aspects of their personal passions that could be monetized, and were able to restructure their lives in ways that gave them greater freedom and fulfillment.
- Here, finally, distilled into one easy-to-use guide, are the most valuable lessons from those who've learned how to turn what they do into a gateway to self-fulfillment.
- It's all about finding the intersection between your "expertise"—even if you don't consider it such—and what other people will pay for.
- You don't need an MBA, a business plan or even employees.
- All you need is a product or service that springs from what you love to do anyway, people willing to pay, and a way to get paid..

WHAT OTHERS SAY:

"Thoughtful, funny, and compulsively readable, this guide shows how ordinary people can build solid livings, with independence and purpose, on their own terms."—Gretchen Rubin, author of the #1 New York Times bestseller The Happiness Project

"Delivers exactly what a new entrepreneur needs: road-tested, effective and exceptionally pragmatic advice for starting a new business on a shoestring." - Pamela Slim, author of Escape from Cubicle Nation.

53
INFINITE POSSIBILITIES
AUTHOR: MIKE DOOLEY

We are all filled with infinite possibilities, and it's time to explore how powerful we truly are.

Amazon (US) star rating: 4.7 ★
Number of Amazon (US) reviews: 510
Published: 2009

About the author:

Mike Dooley is a former PricewaterhouseCoopers international tax consultant turned entrepreneur.

He's the founder of an online philosophical Adventurers Club that's now home to more than 800,000 members from 182 countries.

He is the author of the New York Times bestsellers Leveraging the Universe and Infinite Possibilities.
Mike lives what he teaches and has spoken to audiences in 132 cities, thirty-four countries, and six continents.

tut.com IG @mikedooleytut

more about
INFINITE POSSIBILITIES

- The New York Times bestselling author, teacher, and speaker provides the next step beyond his immensely popular Notes from the Universe trilogy with this special 10th anniversary edition of the modern classic that contains even more enriching wisdom for living an abundant, joyous life.
- We create our own reality, our own fate, and our own luck.
- We are all filled with infinite possibilities, and it's time to explore how powerful we truly are.
- With clear-eyed and masterful prose, Infinite Possibilities effortlessly reveals our true spiritual nature and exactly what it takes to find true happiness and fulfillment.
- Witty and intelligent, this is "the perfect book at the perfect time. It is full of wisdom, answers, and guidance—a unique combination that is guaranteed to help anyone during times of change and transition" (Ariane de Bonvoisin, bestselling author of The First 30 Days).
- This tenth anniversary edition features a new foreword by Bob Proctor and a new introduction from the author.

WHAT OTHERS SAY:

Life changing. If you're a believer that your thoughts and beliefs can create the things in your life, whether material things or whatever it is that will bring you happiness, this book will become your bible.

The most profound book I've ever read! It has changed my life in such a positive way! If your life isn't everything (and I mean *everything* you want it to be), then read this book.

54
INFLUENCE

AUTHOR: ROBERT CIALDINI

The Psychology of Persuasion

Amazon (US) star rating: 4.6 ★
Number of Amazon (US) reviews: 5,139
Published: 2007

About the author:

Dr. Robert Cialdini has spent his entire career researching the science of influence (what leads people to say "Yes" to requests), earning him an international reputation as an expert in the fields of persuasion, compliance, and negotiation.

The results of his research, his ensuing articles, and New York Times bestselling books have earned him an acclaimed reputation as a respected scientist and engaging storyteller.

influenceatwork.com

more about INFLUENCE

- The widely adopted, now classic book on influence and persuasion—a major national and international bestseller with more than four million copies sold!
- In this highly acclaimed New York Times bestseller, Dr. Robert B. Cialdini—the seminal expert in the field of influence and persuasion—explains the psychology of why people say yes and how to apply these principles ethically in business and everyday situations.
- You'll learn the six universal principles of influence and how to use them to become a skilled persuader—and, just as importantly, how to defend yourself against dishonest influence attempts:
  Reciprocation, Commitment and Consistency, Social Proof, Liking, Authority, Scarcity
- Understanding and applying the six principles ethically is cost-free and deceptively easy.
- Backed by Dr. Cialdini's 35 years of evidence-based, peer-reviewed scientific research—as well as by a three-year field study on what moves people to change behavior—Influence is a comprehensive guide to using these principles effectively to amplify your ability to change the behavior of others.

WHAT OTHERS SAY:

The material in Cialdini's Influence is a proverbial gold mine. (Journal of Social and Clinical Psychology)

This book can't be summarized. It can only be very, very strongly recommended. Buy it now.

55
INFLUENCER
AUTHOR: BRITTANY HENNESSY

A guide through core influencer principles

Amazon (US) star rating: 4.6 ★
Number of Amazon (US) reviews: 686
Published: 2018

More about the author:

Brittany is the co-founder & Chief Relationship Officer at CARBON AUGUST, an influencer development platform serving creators, performers, and entrepreneurs.
Brittany was the first Senior Director, Influencer Strategy & Talent Partnerships at Hearst Magazines Digital Media where she secured fashion & beauty influencers for Cosmopolitan, Harper's Bazaar, Elle, Esquire, Town & Country, Seventeen, Good Housekeeping, and other titles across the digital portfolio.
She was also the first Associate Director, Social Strategy & Influence at Horizon Media where she secured comedy and parenting influencers for top brands in the entertainment, spirits, CPG, and automotive categories.
Brittany was named to Talking Influence's 2018 Top Industry Player list, is a member of the Real-Time Academy of Short Form Arts and Sciences where she judges the annual Shorty Awards and the Shorty Social Good Awards, and was also a judge of the 2019 Influencer Marketing Awards.
brittanyhennessy.com   IG @mrsbrittanyhennessy

more about
INFLUENCER

- If you've ever scrolled through your Instagram feed and thought, I wear clothes, eat avocado toast and like sunsets, why can't someone pay me to live my best life? This book is for you.
- Every one of your favorite influencers started with zero followers and had to make a lot of mistakes to get where they are today—earning more money each year than their parents made in the last decade.
- But to become a top creator, you need to understand the strategies behind the Insta-ready lifestyle . . .
- She has unrivaled insight into where the branded content industry was, where it is, and where it's going. In this book she'll reveal how to:

1. Build an audience and keep them engaged
2. Package your brand and pitch your favorite companies
3. Monetize your influence and figure out how much to charge

- Whether you're just starting out or you're ready for bigger campaigns, Hennessy guides you through core influencer principles.
- From creating content worth double tapping and using hashtags to get discovered, to understanding FTC rules and delivering metrics, she'll show you how to elevate your profile, embrace your edge, and make money—all while doing what you love.

WHAT OTHERS SAY:

"I highly advise anyone who has an interest in life online to get this book, sit down, and take notes because you're going to want to hear what Brittany has to say."
-Iskra Lawrence, Aerie Model and Instagram star

Read this book in a day and it has a ton of great information - all the do's and don'ts, how to build your brand, and how to package it.

56
THE LEAN START-UP
AUTHOR: ERIC RIES

How Today's Entrepreneurs Use Continuous Innovation to Create Radically Successful Businesses

Amazon (US) star rating: 4.5 ★

Number of Amazon (US) reviews: 6,06w

Published: 2011

About the author:

ERIC RIES is an entrepreneur and author of the popular blog Startup Lessons Learned.
He co-founded and served as CTO of IMVU, his third startup, and has had plenty of startup failures along the way.
He is a frequent speaker at business events, has advised a number of startups, large companies, and venture capital firms on business and product strategy, and is an Entrepreneur-in-Residence at Harvard Business School.
His Lean Startup methodology has been written about in the New York Times, the Wall Street Journal, the Harvard Business Review, the Huffington Post, and many blogs.
He lives in San Francisco.

theleanstartup.com

more about
THE LEAN START-UP

- Most startups fail. But many of those failures are preventable. The Lean Startup is a new approach being adopted across the globe, changing the way companies are built and new products are launched.
- Eric Ries defines a startup as an organization dedicated to creating something new under conditions of extreme uncertainty.
- This is just as true for one person in a garage or a group of seasoned professionals in a Fortune 500 boardroom. What they have in common is a mission to penetrate that fog of uncertainty to discover a successful path to a sustainable business.
- Inspired by lessons from lean manufacturing, it relies on "validated learning," rapid scientific experimentation, as well as a number of counter-intuitive practices that shorten product development cycles, measure actual progress without resorting to vanity metrics, and learn what customers really want. It enables a company to shift directions with agility, altering plans inch by inch, minute by minute.
- Rather than wasting time creating elaborate business plans, it offer a way to test their vision continuously, to adapt and adjust before it's too late.

WHAT OTHERS SAY:
I have read countless management, business and self-development books and I can honestly say this is the first one that I have truly used like a workbook.

If you are an entrepreneur, read this book. If you are thinking about becoming an entrepreneur, read this book. If you are just curious about entrepreneurship, read this book.

57
LET IT GO (MEMOIR)
AUTHORS: DAME STEPHANIE SHIRLEY & RICHARD ASKWITH

Dame Stephanie Shirley's Extraordinary Story - from Refugee to Entrepreneur to Philanthropist

Amazon (US) star rating: 4.8 ★
Number of Amazon (US) reviews: 64
Published: 2019

About the authors:
Dame Stephanie Shirley is a British businesswoman, technology pioneer, and philanthropist.
She founded a software company called Freelance Programmers, and transferred ownership of the company to her staff, making 70 women millionaires.
Shirley has dedicated most of her life and wealth to advancing Autism research and STEM subjects.
She co-founded the Oxford Internet Institute and was President of the British Computer Society.
She was named by BBC Radio 4's Women's Hour as one of the 100 most powerful women in the UK.
Richard Askwith is a Northamptonshire-based journalist and author whose passions include running, outdoor adventure and the traditions and ordinary people of the English countryside.
steveshirley.com   IG @damestephanie_

more about
LET IT GO (MEMOIR)

- A moving memoir from a woman who made a fortune in a man's world and then gave it all away...soon to be turned into a film.
- In 1962, Stephanie 'Steve' Shirley created a software company when the concept of software barely existed. Freelance Programmers employed women to work on complex projects such as Concorde's black box recorder from the comfort of their own home.
- Shirley empowered a generation of women in technology, giving them unheard of freedom to choose their own hours and manage their own workloads.
- The business thrived and Shirley gradually transferred ownership to her staff, creating 70 millionaires in the process.
- Let It Go explores Shirley's trail blazing career as an entrepreneur but it also charts her incredible personal story - her dramatic arrival in England as an unaccompanied Kindertransport refugee during World War Two and the tragic loss of her only child who suffered severely from Autism.
- Today, Dame Stephanie Shirley is one of Britain's leading philanthropists, devoting most of her time, energy and wealth to charities that are close to her heart.
- Shirley tells her inspirational story and explains why giving her wealth away - letting it go - has brought her infinitely more happiness and fulfilment than acquiring it in the first place.

WHAT OTHERS SAY:
'There is an entire business course in this book...but more important, this engrossing story of an extraordinary life is filled with lessons in what it means to be human' - Financial Times

A must read for any woman who has failed. She was just an average 20 something, who with determination, builds her empire. Near-failures included! So much hope in this story.

58
LIMITLESS
AUTHOR: JIM KWIK

Upgrade Your Brain, Learn Anything Faster, and Unlock Your Exceptional Life

Amazon (US) star rating: 4.7 ★
Number of Amazon (US) reviews: 4,587
Published: 2020

Jim Kwik is a world-renowned expert in memory improvement, brain optimization, and accelerated learning.
After a childhood brain injury left him learning-challenged, Kwik created strategies to dramatically enhance his mental performance.
He has since dedicated his life to helping others unleash their true genius and brainpower.
For over two decades, he has served as a brain coach to students, seniors, entrepreneurs, and educators.
His work has touched a who's who of Hollywood elite, professional athletes, political leaders, and business magnates, with corporate clients.
Through keynote speeches, he reaches in-person audiences totaling more than 200,000 every year.
He is the host of the acclaimed "Kwik Brain" podcast, which is consistently the top educational training show on iTunes.
His online courses are used by students in 195 countries (Kwiklearning).
Kwik, an advocate for brain health and global education, is also a philanthropist with projects ranging from Alzheimer's research to funding the creation of schools from Guatemala to Kenya, providing health care, clean water, and learning for children in need. His mission: No brain left behind.
jimkwik.com   IG @jimkwik

more about LIMITLESS

- JIM KWIK, the world's #1 brain coach, has written the owner's manual for mental expansion and brain fitness.
- Limitless gives people the ability to accomplish more--more productivity, more transformation, more personal success and business achievement--by changing their Mindset, Motivation, and Methods.
- These "3 M's" live in the pages of Limitless along with practical techniques that unlock the superpowers of your brain and change your habits.
- For over 25 years, Jim Kwik has worked closely with successful men and women who are at the top in their fields as actors, athletes, CEOs, and business leaders from all walks of life to unlock their true potential.
- In this groundbreaking book, he reveals the science-based practices and field-tested tips to accelerate self learning, communication, memory, focus, recall, and speed reading, to create fast, hard results.
- Limitless helps you learn anything faster, and once you've done that, there is nothing holding you back from your dreams.

WHAT OTHERS SAY:

"There's a whole science behind brain fitness, memory enhancement, and mental acuity, and Jim Kwik is the ultimate guide."
— Lisa Mosconi, Ph.D., Director of the Women's Brain Initiative, author of Brain Food and The XX Brain

I bought this book wanting to learn how to read faster and enhance my memory. I got more than that.

I've been a long time self-empowerment reader and podcast listener. The formula and teachings in this book are next level.

59
MADE TO STICK
AUTHORS: CHIP & DAN HEATH
Why Some Ideas Survive and Others Die

Amazon (US) star rating: 4.6 ★
Number of Amazon (US) reviews: 1,967
Published: 2006

About the author:

Chip Heath is a professor at Stanford Graduate School of Business, teaching courses on business strategy and organizations. He has consulted with clients ranging from Google and Gap to The Nature Conservancy and the American Heart Association. His parents are just happy that their sons are playing well together.
Dan Heath is a Senior Fellow at Duke University's CASE center, which supports social entrepreneurs.
Previously, Dan worked as a researcher and case writer for Harvard Business School. In the late 1990s, Dan co-founded an innovative publishing company called Thinkwell, which for almost 25 years has been producing a line of online college textbooks that feature video lectures from some of the country's top professors.

heathbrothers.com

more about MADE TO STICK

- The instant classic about why some ideas thrive, why others die, and how to improve your idea's chances—essential reading in the "fake news" era.
- In Made to Stick, Chip and Dan Heath reveal the anatomy of ideas that stick and explain ways to make ideas stickier, such as applying the human scale principle, using the Velcro Theory of Memory, and creating curiosity gaps.
- Along the way, we discover that sticky messages of all kinds—from the infamous "kidney theft ring" hoax to a coach's lessons on sportsmanship to a vision for a new product at Sony—draw their power from the same six traits.
- Made to Stick will transform the way you communicate.
- It's a fast-paced tour of success stories (and failures): the Nobel Prize-winning scientist who drank a glass of bacteria to prove a point about stomach ulcers; the charities who make use of the Mother Teresa Effect; the elementary-school teacher whose simulation actually prevented racial prejudice.
- Provocative, eye-opening, and often surprisingly funny,
- Made to Stick shows us the vital principles of winning ideas—and tells us how we can apply these rules to making our own messages stick.

WHAT OTHERS SAY:

An easy-to-use formula on how to identify and create successful, "sticky" and transformative ideas.

This book is without a doubt one of the most useful things I've read this year.

Essentially, sticky ideas are never a matter of happenstance, but all share six common traits.

60
MARKETING MADE SIMPLE

*AUTHORS: DONALD MILLER &
DR JJ PETERSON*

A Step-by-Step StoryBrand Guide for Any Business

Amazon (US) star rating: 4.8 ★

Number of Amazon (US) reviews: 416

Published: 2020

About the author:

Donald Miller is the CEO of StoryBrand, the cohost of the Building a StoryBrand Podcast, and the author of several books

Every year he helps more than 3,000 business leaders clarify their brand message.

Don is widely considered one of the most entertaining and informative speakers in the world.

His audiences are challenged to lean into their own story, creatively develop and execute the story of their team, and understand the story of their customers so they can serve them with passion.

Don's thoughts on story have deeply influenced leaders and teams for Pantene, Chick-fil-A, Steelcase, Intel, Prime Lending, Zaxby's, and thousands more.

Don lives in Nashville, Tennessee, with his wife, Betsy, and their chocolate lab, Lucy.

*storybrand.com   IG @storybrand_*

more about
MARKETING MADE SIMPLE

- Lots of marketing agencies will sell you new logos, color schemes, and brand guidelines followed by Facebook ads and slick landing pages.
- But without a sales funnel in place, most of that stuff won't work.
- If you've been wasting money on marketing, this book will help you stop that waste in its tracks.
- Follow the easy-to-understand blueprint in Marketing Made Simple to increase sales, grow your mission, and connect with customers.
- Every day, brands lose millions of dollars simply because they do not have a clear message that tells consumers who they are and what value they will add to their customers' lives.
- To solve this dilemma, Donald Miller wrote Building a StoryBrand, which has become the quintessential guide for anyone looking to craft or strengthen their brand's message.
- Now, Don is taking it a step further with this five-part checklist that helps marketing professionals and business owners apply the StoryBrand messaging framework across key customer touchpoints to effectively develop, strengthen, and communicate their brand's story to the marketplace.

WHAT OTHERS SAY:

I desperately needed this book and absolutely consumed the content. I bought the audiobook first but the content was so rich and detailed, I bought the print version as well.

Donald Miller has made a huge positive impact on my business thru his books. This one and his previous book. I highly recommend getting both and signing up for his daily tips too. This guy is a marketing genius and he has a way of making it so you can be too.

61
MAY CAUSE MIRACLES

AUTHOR: GABRIELLE BERNSTEIN

A 40-Day Guidebook of Subtle Shifts for Radical Change and Unlimited Happiness

Amazon (US) star rating: 4.5 ★

Number of Amazon (US) reviews: 1,019

Published: 2012

About the author:

GABRIELLE BERNSTEIN, a member of Oprah's Super Soul 100, the #1 New York Times bestselling author of eight books, the cofounder of the Women's Entrepreneurial Network, a nonprofit professional organization that connects female entrepreneurs.

Her mission is to help you crack open to a spiritual relationship of your own understanding so that you can live in alignment with your true purpose, too!

She created the Spirit Junkie App to help you start the morning right with inspiring affirmations every day.

Since 2004, Gabrielle has been on the speaking circuit, lecturing and conducting motivational workshops.

gabbybernstein.com   IG @gabbybernstein

more about
MAY CAUSE MIRACLES

- A practical and fun 40-day guidebook of subtle shifts for radical change and unlimited happiness.
- Are you ready to work miracles?
- Gabrielle Bernstein believes that simple, consistent shifts in our thinking and actions can lead to the miraculous in all aspects of our daily lives, including our relationships, finances, bodies, and self-image.
- In this inspiring guide, Gabrielle offers an exciting plan for releasing fear and allowing gratitude, forgiveness, and love to flow through us without fail.
- All of which, ultimately, will lead to breathtaking lives of abundance, acceptance, appreciation, and happiness.
- With May Cause Miracles, readers can expect incredible transformation in 40 powerful days: simply by adding up subtle shifts to create miraculous change.

WHAT OTHERS SAY:

This book has changed my life.
This book is not a normal book that you just read from cover to cover. It is a 6 week course in book form.

I'm on the last week of this book but it truly did make me look at life differently. Her book showed me how gratefulness and a positive mind are really beneficial. And how the ego controls your life and thoughts in a bad way. Definitely made me aware of my bad negative thought processes.

This book is a miracle creator! I enjoy this so much. I'm on day 36 and I don't want it to end so I'll be starting over

62
MEASURE WHAT MATTERS

AUTHOR: JOHN DOERR

Objectives & Key Results (OKR's): The Simple Idea That Drives 10x Growth

Amazon (US) star rating: 4.5 ★

Number of Amazon (US) reviews: 1,707

Published: 2018

About the author:

John Doerr is an engineer, acclaimed venture capitalist, and the chairman of Kleiner Perkins.

For 37 years, John has served entrepreneurs with ingenuity and optimism, helping them build disruptive companies and bold teams. In 2018, he authored Measure What Matters, a handbook for setting and achieving audacious goals. Through his book and platform, WhatMatters.com, he shares valuable lessons from some of the most fearless innovators of our time.

John was an original investor and board member at Google and Amazon, helping to create more than half a million jobs and the world's second and third most valuable companies. He's passionate about encouraging leaders to reimagine the future, from transforming healthcare to advancing applications of machine learning. Outside of Kleiner Perkins, John works with social entrepreneurs for change in public education, the climate crisis, and global poverty. John serves on the board of the Obama Foundation and ONE.org.

whatmatters.com

more about

MEASURE WHAT MATTERS

- In the fall of 1999, John Doerr met with the founders of a start-up whom he'd just given $12.5 million, the biggest investment of his career.
- Larry Page and Sergey Brin had amazing technology, entrepreneurial energy, and sky-high ambitions, but no real business plan.
- For Google to succeed, Page and Brin had to learn how to make tough choices on priorities while keeping their team on track. They'd have to know when to pull the plug on losing propositions, to fail fast. And they needed timely, relevant data to track their progress—to measure what mattered.
- Doerr taught them about a proven approach to operating excellence: Objectives and Key Results. Later, as a venture capitalist, Doerr shared Grove's brainchild with more than fifty companies. Wherever the process was faithfully practiced, it worked.
- In this goal-setting system, objectives define what we seek to achieve; key results are how those top-priority goals will be attained with specific, measurable actions within a set time frame. Everyone's goals, from entry level to CEO, are transparent to the entire organization.

WHAT OTHERS SAY:
"Whether you're a seasoned CEO or a first-time entrepreneur,
you'll find valuable lessons, tools, and inspiration. I'm glad John
invested the time to share these ideas with the world." Reid Hoffman,
LinkedIn cofounder, author of The Start-up of You

I read it in one sitting and plan to re-read, dissect and map out my
businesses Objectives and Key Results

63

THE MILLION DOLLAR ONE PERSON BUSINESS

AUTHOR: ELAINE POFELDT

Make Great Money. Work the Way You Like. Have the Life You Want.

Amazon (US) star rating: 4.5 ★
Number of Amazon (US) reviews: 216
Published: 2018

About the author:
Elaine Pofeldt is an independent journalist who specializes in small business, entrepreneurship and careers. Her work has appeared in FORTUNE, Money, CNBC, Inc., Forbes, Crain's New York Business and other business publications and she is a contributor to the Economist Intelligence Unit.

As a senior editor at FORTUNE Small Business, where she worked for eight years, Elaine was twice nominated for the National Magazine Award for her features and ran the magazine's annual business plan completion. During her time at FSB, she ran the magazine's website, fsb.com, for four years, building its traffic to two to five million page views a month.

Elaine graduated from Yale University with a BA in English. She lives in in New Jersey with her husband and their four children and in her free time enjoys taekwondo, yoga and running.

elainepofeldt.com   *IG@milliondollaronepersonbusiness*

more about
THE MILLION DOLLAR ONE PERSON BUSINESS

- The rise of one-million-dollar, one-person businesses in the past five years is the biggest trend in employment today, offering the widest range of people the most ways to earn a living while having the lifestyles they want.
- Elaine Pofeldt explains how to identify, launch, grow, and reinvent the business, showing how an individual can generate $1 million in revenue-something only larger small companies have done before.
- Many owners have never learned how to create a high-revenue, high-profit business without adding a lot of overhead. It's not something you'll learn in school or even from other business owners.
- The Million-Dollar, One-Person Business closes that gap. It offers a road map to creating a seven-figure, ultra-lean firm by sharing the strategies of entrepreneurs who have approached and hit $1 million in revenue before adding employees. From their experiences, you'll learn how to come up with the right business idea, how to develop concrete strategies you can use to turn your vision into reality, and how to scale your revenues and profits once they start rolling in.
- Once you know how to create a million-dollar, one-person business, you'll have many possibilities in front of you. Some owners choose to keep their businesses small, building them around a lifestyle they love. Others decide to follow the path outlined in my book, Scaling Up, and create fast-growing, job-creating firms.
- No matter which route you choose, you'll have exciting options.

WHAT OTHERS SAY:
"In an era when freelancing, small office/home office, and one-person businesses are exploding, a definitive guidebook for any would-be entrepreneur who is looking to brainstorm, grow, sell, and succeed."
—Gene Marks, CPA at the Marks Group PC

I kept reading certain sections out loud to my husband. I could not put this book down!

64
MINDSET

AUTHOR: DR CAROL DECK

The New Psychology of Success.
Almost every area of human endeavor
can be dramatically influenced by how
we think about our talents and abilities.

Amazon (US) star rating: 4.5 ★
Number of Amazon (US) reviews: 5,763
Published: 2007

About the author:
Carol S. Dweck, Ph.D., is widely regarded as one of the world's leading
researchers in the fields of personality, social psychology, and
developmental psychology.
She is the Lewis and Virginia Eaton Professor of Psychology at
Stanford University, has been elected to the American Academy of
Arts and Sciences and the National Academy of Sciences, and has
won nine lifetime achievement awards for her research.
She addressed the United Nations on the eve of their new global
development plan and has advised governments on educational and
economic policies.
Her work has been featured in almost every major national
publication, and she has appeared on Today, Good Morning America,
and 20/20.
She lives with her husband in Palo Alto, California.

more about MINDSET

- After decades of research, world-renowned Stanford University psychologist Carol S. Dweck, Ph.D., discovered a simple but groundbreaking idea: the power of mindset.
- In this brilliant book, she shows how success in school, work, sports, the arts, and almost every area of human endeavor can be dramatically influenced by how we think about our talents and abilities.
- People with a fixed mindset—those who believe that abilities are fixed —are less likely to flourish than those with a growth mindset—those who believe that abilities can be developed.
- Mindset reveals how great parents, teachers, managers, and athletes can put this idea to use to foster outstanding accomplishment.
- In this edition, Dweck offers new insights into her now famous and broadly embraced concept.
- She introduces a phenomenon she calls false growth mindset and guides people toward adopting a deeper, truer growth mindset.
- She also expands the mindset concept beyond the individual, applying it to the cultures of groups and organizations.
- With the right mindset, you can motivate those you lead, teach, and love—to transform their lives and your own.

WHAT OTHERS SAY:
"Everyone should read this book."
—Chip Heath and Dan Heath, authors of *Made to Stick*

"One of the most influential books ever about motivation."
—Po Bronson, author of *NurtureShock*

"If you manage people or are a parent (which is a form of managing people), drop everything and read Mindset."
—Guy Kawasaki, author of *The Art of the Start 2.0*

65
THE MIRACLE MORNING
AUTHOR: HAL ELROD

The 6 Habits that Will Transform Your Life Before 8am

Amazon (US) star rating: 4.5 ★
Number of Amazon (US) reviews: 8,050
First published: 2012

About the author:
Hal Elrod is on a mission to Elevate the Consciousness of Humanity, One Person at a Time.
With 'The Miracle Morning' which has been translated into 37 languages, has over 3,000 five-star reviews and has impacted the lives of over 2m people in more than 70 countries... he is doing exactly that.
What's incredible is that Hal literally died at age 20. His car was hit head-on by a drunk driver at 70 miles per hour, his heart stopped beating for 6 minutes, he broke 11 bones and woke up after being in a coma for 6 days to be told by his doctors that he would probably never walk again. Not only did Hal walk, he ran a 52-mile ultra-marathon!
Then, in November of 2016, Hal nearly died again - his kidneys, lungs, and heart were failing, and he was diagnosed with a rare, and very aggressive form of cancer and given a 30% chance of living.
After enduring the most difficult year of his life, Hal is now cancer-free and furthering his mission as the founder of The Miracle Morning book series, host of the "Achieve Your Goals" podcast, creator of the Best Year Ever [Blueprint] LIVE event, and Executive Producer of The Miracle Morning MOVIE - a documentary that reveals the morning rituals of some of the world's most successful people.
Hal is grateful to be alive and living his mission alongside his wife and their two young children in Austin, TX.
miraclemorning.com IG @hal_elrod

more about
THE MIRACLE MORNING

- What's being widely regarded as "one of the most life changing books ever written" may be the simplest approach to achieving everything you've ever wanted, and faster than you ever thought possible.
- What if you could wake up tomorrow and any—or EVERY—area of your life was beginning to transform?
- What would you change?
- The Miracle Morning is already transforming the lives of tens of thousands of people around the world by showing them how to wake up each day with more ENERGY, MOTIVATION, and FOCUS to take your life to the next level. It's been right here in front of us all along, but this book has finally brought it to life.
- Are you ready? The next chapter of YOUR life—the most extraordinary life you've ever imagined—is about to begin.

WHAT OTHERS SAY:

"Hal Elrod is a genius and his book The Miracle Morning has been magical in my life. What Hal has done is taken the best practices, developed over centuries of human consciousness development, and condensed the 'best of the best' into a daily morning ritual. A ritual that is now part of my day."
—Robert Kiyosaki, bestselling author of Rich Dad Poor Dad

Half way through the book and I feel a massive difference in my approach to life already.

I do not have enough words to say how much this book has change the path of my life. After I found this book, I found Hal's podcasts and from there on his Facebook group.

66
NEW STARTUP MINDSET
AUTHOR: SANDRA SHPILBERG

Ten Mindset Shifts to Build the Company of Your Dreams

Amazon (US) star rating: 4.8 ★

Number of Amazon (US) reviews: 100

Published: 2020

About the author:

Sandra Shpilberg is the founder and CEO of Seeker Health, a leading digital patient finding platform. She's currently the CEO of Adnexi, a disease intelligence platform.

She has been named a Top 40 Healthcare Transformer and was a featured speaker at the 2018 South by Southwest conference.

Shpilberg writes for the Huffington Post and has been published in American Economist and Lancet. Sandra also served as editor for Here My Home Once Stood: A Holocaust Memoir by Moyshe Rekhtman.

Her writing has also been featured in The Sleep Revolution by Arianna Huffington. She was born in Uruguay and now lives in California.

sandrashpilberg.com   IG @sandrashpilberg

more about
NEW STARTUP MINDSET

- This book will show you a new way to succeed as an entrepreneur!
- The provocative startup tale of success exposes Silicon Valley's startup myths and sets forth a new approach for aspiring and current founders to build companies that make an impact.
- In New Startup Mindset, Sandra Shpilberg, founder and CEO of Seeker Health, introduces a new mindset for starting and building a successful company.
- Shpilberg shows that Silicon Valley's startup formula—a few young male cofounders attempting to build a unicorn funded by venture capital—is a broken system that puts excessive emphasis on hype and improbable outsized outcomes, disregards real results such as revenue and profit, and promotes limiting beliefs for the next generation of entrepreneurs.
- In 2015, Shpilberg founded Seeker Health, a digital patient-finding platform. The company grew rapidly to serve over sixty biotechnology companies, connect millions of patients with serious diseases to clinical trials, and achieve great financial success.
- From the start, Shpilberg did almost everything differently than the blazed path: she chose to be a solo founder,, didn't accept outside funding, led development of software despite not being a programmer, and charged customers from month one.
- Instead of creating hype about fundraising based on fictitious valuations, Shpilberg focused on customer needs, yielding a startup with revenue, profit, and impact; and in September 2018, a large life science services company acquired her startup while she was still the sole owner.

WHAT OTHERS SAY:
If you're thinking about starting a business, "New Startup Mindset" is THE book to read. Sandra's story offers lots of practical wisdom and inspiring examples delivered with even more heart.

She had me at "You don't need a unicorn and you can sleep 8 hours a day! his is one of those books I know I will refer to often.

67
THE ONE MINUTE MILLIONAIRE
AUTHORS: MARK VICTOR HANSEN & ROBERT G ALLEN

TINY CHANGES, REMARKABLE RESULTS
An Easy and Proven Way to Build Good Habits and Break Bad Ones

Amazon (US) star rating: 4.5 ★
Number of Amazon (US) reviews: 414
First published:

About the authors:
Mark Victor Hansen is probably best known as the co-author for the Chicken Soup for the Soulbook series and brand, setting world records in book sales, with over 500 millions books sold.

Mark also worked his way into a worldwide spotlight as a sought-after keynote speaker, and entrepreneurial marketing maven, creating a stream of successful people who have created massive success for themselves through Mark's unique teachings and wisdom.

Robert G. Allen is an author and mentor beloved for his down-to-earth style and highly effective systems. His purpose in life is to help you achieve your dreams.

He's been teaching and writing towards that purpose for forty years. His first book, the colossal #1 NYT bestseller, Nothing Down: How to Buy Real Estate with Little or No Money Down, is the largest selling real estate investment book in history, and established Bob as one of the most influential investment advisors of all time In his following bestsellers, Creating Wealth and The Challenge, he expanded on his highly profitable real estate techniques and philosophy.

markvictorhansen.com   *www.robertallen.com*

more about
THE ONE MINUTE MILLIONAIRE

- Two mega-bestselling authors with decades of experience in teaching people how to achieve extraordinary wealth and success share their secrets. Mark Victor Hansen, co-creator of the phenomenal Chicken Soup for the Soul series, and Robert G. Allen, one of the world's foremost financial experts, have helped thousands of people become millionaires. Now it's your turn.
- Is it possible to make a million dollars in only one minute? The answer just might surprise you. The One Minute Millionaire is an entirely new approach, a life-changing "millionaire system" that will teach you:

1. Create wealth even when you have nothing to start with.
2. Overcome fears so you can take reasonable risks.
3. Use the power of leverage to build wealth rapidly.
4. Use "one minute" habits to build wealth over the long term.

- The One Minute Millionaire is a revolutionary approach to building wealth and a powerful program for self-discovery as well.
- Here are two books in one, fiction and nonfiction, designed to address two kinds of learning so that you can fully integrate these lessons.
- On the right-hand pages, you will find the fictional story of a woman who has to make a million dollars in ninety days or lose her two children forever. The left-hand pages give the practical, step-by-step nonfiction strategies and techniques that actually work in the real world. You'll find more than one hundred nuts-and-bolts "Millionaire Minutes," each one a concise and invaluable lesson with specific techniques for creating wealth.

WHAT OTHERS SAY:
Change your life today. I bought this book on a whim and it was one of the best decisions I've ever made.

This mega-selling twosome offers a pep talk on how just about anybody can make big money.

68
OUTLIERS
AUTHOR: MALCOLM GLADWELL

What makes high-achievers different?
An intellectual journey through the world of
"outliers"- the best and the brightest, the most
famous and the most successful.

Amazon (US) star rating: 4.6 ★

Number of Amazon (US) reviews: 11,570

Published: 2011

About the author:

Malcolm Gladwell is the author of five New York Times bestsellers —
The Tipping Point, Blink, Outliers, What the Dog Saw, and David and
Goliath.

He is also the co-founder of Pushkin Industries, an audio content
company that produces the podcasts Revisionist History, which
reconsiders things both overlooked and misunderstood, and Broken
Record, where he, Rick Rubin, and Bruce Headlam interview
musicians across a wide range of genres.

Gladwell has been included in the TIME 100 Most Influential People
list and touted as one of Foreign Policy's Top Global Thinkers.

www.gladwellbooks.com IG @malcolmgladwell

more about
OUTLIERS

- In this stunning new book, Malcolm Gladwell takes us on an intellectual journey through the world of "outliers"--the best and the brightest, the most famous and the most successful.
- He asks the question: what makes high-achievers different?
- His answer is that we pay too much attention to what successful people are like, and too little attention to where they are from: that is, their culture, their family, their generation, and the idiosyncratic experiences of their upbringing.
- Along the way he explains the secrets of software billionaires, what it takes to be a great soccer player, why Asians are good at math, and what made the Beatles the greatest rock band.
- Brilliant and entertaining, Outliers is a landmark work that will simultaneously delight and illuminate.

WHAT OTHERS SAY:
Outliers is riveting science, self-help, and entertainment, all in one book. Gregory Kirschling, Entertainment Weekly

Gladwell argues that success is tightly married to opportunity and time on task. He states that it takes approximately 10,000 hours to master something and that gives me comfort.

Fascinating and thought-provoking

69
THE POWER OF RECEIVING

AUTHOR: AMANDA OWEN

A Revolutionary Approach to Giving Yourself the Life You Want and Deserve

Amazon (US) star rating: 4.8 ★
Number of Amazon (US) reviews: 107
Published: 2010

About the author:

Amanda Owen is a consultant-coach in the areas of spirituality, empowerment, and self-improvement, and has created the transformative Receive and Manifest workshops.
Her research over the last twenty years into the nature of receptivity, along with her studies in quantum theory and Buddhism, led her to develop a system that helps people create the lives they want.
In addition to her work as a writer and speaker, Amanda is an independent scholar of women's history, specializing in the American women's suffrage movement.
She is a co-founder and the Executive Director of the Justice Bell Foundation.
She is currently writing a book about the Justice Bell and is working with filmmaker Martha Wheelock on a documentary about the Justice Bell and the women's suffrage movement.
amandaowen.com IG *@amanda.owen*

more about
THE POWER OF RECEIVING

- Once in a blue moon an idea comes along that once heard seems so obvious that you wonder why somebody hasn't written about it before.
- A Revolutionary Approach to Giving Yourself the Life You Want and Deserve presents a new paradigm for the 21st century-a philosophy that values receiving as much as giving and demonstrates that giving is enhanced when receiving is embraced.
- With the formula: Believe + Receive = Achieve, The Power of Receiving presents a wholly original yet easily accessible road map for people to follow, showing readers how to restore balance to their over-extended lives and attract the life they desire and deserve.
- Inspiring stories are featured about people who have experienced life-altering results after becoming skilled Receivers, including Ken who regained his hearing after a devastating hearing-loss, Julie who met the man she would later marry, and Don who received an extra $1,000 a month in his pay check.
- Based on over twenty years of research into the nature of receptivity and its link to manifestation, The Power of Receiving offers a unique vision for anyone seeking to create greater reciprocity in their relationships and more harmony and abundance in their lives.

WHAT OTHERS SAY:
Eye-Opening and Life-Changing.
There's a reason this book has 5 stars!

Keep Recommending this Book to Anyone Who Will Listen!

This book is a must-read for anyone who has ever wondered why they've not been able to achieve the kind of life they want to live.

70
PROFIT FIRST
AUTHOR: MIKE MICHAELOWITZ
Your Business from a Cash-Eating Monster to a Money-Making Machine

Amazon (US) star rating: 4.8 ★

Number of Amazon (US) reviews: 3,185

Published: 2017

About the author:

By his 35th birthday MIKE MICHALOWICZ (pronounced mi-'kal-o-wits) had founded and sold two multi-million dollar companies.

Today, Mike leads two new multi-million-dollar ventures, as he tests his latest business research for his books.
He is a former small business columnist for The Wall Street Journal and business makeover specialist on MSNBC.
Mike is a popular main stage keynote speaker on innovative entrepreneurial topics; and is the author of Fix This Next, Clockwork, Profit First, Surge, The Pumpkin Plan and The Toilet Paper Entrepreneur.

Mike is also a guest lecturer for collegiate entrepreneurial programs

mikemichalowicz.com   IG @mikemichalowicz

more about
PROFIT FIRST

- Profit First offers a simple, counterintuitive cash management solution that will help small businesses break out of the doom spiral and achieve instant profitability.
- Conventional accounting uses the logical (albeit, flawed) formula: Sales - Expenses = Profit.
- The problem is, businesses are run by humans, and humans aren't always logical.
- Serial entrepreneur Mike Michalowicz has developed a behavioral approach to accounting to flip the formula: Sales-Profit = Expenses.
- Just as the most effective weight loss strategy is to limit portions by using smaller plates, Michalowicz shows that by taking profit first and apportioning only what remains for expenses, entrepreneurs will transform their businesses from cash-eating monsters to profitable cash cows. Using Michalowicz's Profit First system, readers will learn that:

1. Following 4 simple principles can simplify accounting and make it easier to manage a profitable business by looking at bank account balances.
2. A small, profitable business can be worth much more than a large business surviving on its top line.
3. Businesses that attain early and sustained profitability have a better shot at achieving long-term growth.

- With dozens of case studies, practical, step-by-step advice, and his signature sense of humor, this is the game-changing roadmap for any entrepreneur to make money they always dreamed of.

WHAT OTHERS SAY:

"Quit being a slave to your own business and start making some serious money. Follow Mike's counter-intuitive advice and put profits first." -VERNE HARNISH, author of Scaling Up

The most important business book I own.

71
REWORK

AUTHOR: JASON FRIED, DAVID HEINEMEIER HANSSON

Change the way you work forever. From the founders of Basecamp.

Amazon (US) star rating: 4.5 ★
Number of Amazon (US) reviews: 2,454
Published: 2010

About the authors:

Jason Fried and David Heineeier Hansson are the co-founders of 37signals, a privately-held Chicago-based company committed to building the best web-based tools possible with the least number of features necessary.

37signals' products include Basecamp, Highrise, Backpack, Campfire, Ta-da List, and Writeboard. 37signals also developed and open-sourced the Ruby on Rails programming framework.

37signals' products do less than the competition -- intentionally.

37signals weblog, Signal vs. Noise, is read by over 100,000 people every day.

basecamp.com

more about REWORK

- Most business books give you the same old advice: Write a business plan, study the competition, seek investors, yadda yadda. If you're looking for a book like that, put this one back on the shelf.
- Read it and you'll know why plans are actually harmful, why you don't need outside investors, and why you're better off ignoring the competition.
- The truth is, you need less than you think. You don't need to be a workaholic. You don't need to staff up. You don't need to waste time on paperwork or meetings. You don't even need an office. Those are all just excuses.
- What you really need to do is stop talking and start working. This book shows you the way.
- You'll learn how to be more productive, how to get exposure without breaking the bank, and tons more counterintuitive ideas that will inspire and provoke you.
- With its straightforward language and easy-is-better approach, Rework is the perfect playbook for anyone who's ever dreamed of doing it on their own.
- Hardcore entrepreneurs, small-business owners, people stuck in day jobs they hate, victims of "downsizing," and artists who don't want to starve anymore will all find valuable guidance in these pages.

WHAT OTHERS SAY:

*Jason and David have broken all the rules and won. Again and again they've demonstrated that the regular way isn't necessarily the right way. They just don't say it, they do it. And they do it better than just about anyone has any right to expect. **Seth Godin***

Thought provoking, worth a read to rework your approach to work!

72
ROCKET FUEL
AUTHOR: GINO WICKMAN & MARK WINTERS

The One Essential Combination That Will Get You More of What You Want from Your Business

Amazon (US) star rating: 4.7 ★
Number of Amazon (US) reviews: 472
Published: 2015

About the authors:

Gino Wickman created the Entrepreneurial Operating System(r) (EOS), a system that, helps leaders run better businesses, get better control, have better life balance, and gain more traction. He spends most of his time as an EOS Implementer, working hands-on with the leadership teams of entrepreneurial companies to help them fully implement EOS in their organizations. He is the founder of EOS Worldwide, a growing organization of successful entrepreneurs from a variety of business backgrounds collaborating as certified EOS Implementers to help people throughout the world to experience all the organizational and personal benefits of implementing EOS.

Mark C. Winters is a seasoned professional with over 25 years of entrepreneurial leadership experience. His companies have ranged from raw startups originally drawn up on a napkin, to multi-billion dollar global enterprises such as Procter & Gamble and British Petroleum. This diverse background enables him to identify and apply patterns of success for virtually any business scenario. Mark's passion is helping entrepreneurs get what they want from their business. As a Certified EOS Implementer, he's actively engaged in helping other entrepreneurs implement EOS in their own companies. His ability to connect and guide CEOs to achieve their desired results is highly respected. Mark is known for pursuing business opportunities related to technology and systems that enable the optimization of human/athletic performance, with a special interest in pattern recognition & scoring methodologies.

rocketfuelnow.com

more about
ROCKET FUEL

- Discover the vital relationship that will take your company from "What's next?" to "We have lift-off!"
- Visionaries have groundbreaking ideas. Integrators make those ideas a reality. This explosive combination is the key to getting everything you want out of your business. It worked for Disney. It worked for McDonalds. It can work for you.
- From the author of the bestseller Traction, Rocket Fuel details the integral roles of the Visionary and Integrator and explains how an effective relationship between the two can help your business thrive.
- Offering advice to help Visionary-minded and Integrator-minded individuals find one another, Rocket Fuel also features assessments so you're able to determine whether you're a Visionary or an Integrator.
- Without an Integrator, a Visionary is far less likely to succeed long-term, and realize the company's ultimate goals—likewise, with no Visionary, an Integrator can't rise to his or her full potential. When these two people come together to share their natural talents and innate skill sets, it's like rocket fuel—they have the power to reach new heights for virtually any company or organization.

WHAT OTHERS SAY:

"Rocket Fuel is a powerful model for freeing up entrepreneurial visionaries to do what they do best. Gino and Mark provide a practical gameplan for building an organization that perfectly combines vision and integration."
–Dan Sullivan, President and Founder of Strategic Coach®

It has completely changed my business and provided "Clarity & Freedom". The entire operating system has provided Clarity for everyone to know what it takes to be excellent

73

THE SCIENCE OF MIND MANAGEMENT

AUTHOR: SWAMI MUKUNDANANDA

The quality of our mind determines the quality of the life we lead. It can be our greatest ally or our worst adversary.

Amazon (US) star rating: 4.8 ★
Number of Amazon (US) reviews: 209
Published: 2020

About the author:
Swami Mukundananda is a world-renowned spiritual teacher from India with an educational background from IIT and IIM.
Having learned the Vedic scriptures under the tutelage of Jagadguru Shree Kripaluji Maharaj, he now spends his time explaining the path of true, ever-lasting happiness to people everywhere.
In between his hectic schedule, he writes books and commentaries, records CDs and DVDs, and guides a worldwide congregation of devotees.
Swamiji's lectures are humorous, his arguments are logical and well laid-out, and most of all, his advice is practical.
His lectures are much sought after and include various topics such as conquest of the mind, good health through yoga, meditation, and spirituality, and karm yog for everyday living.
jkyog.org   IG @swami_mukundananda

more about
THE SCIENCE OF MIND MANAGEMENT

- The quality of our mind determines the quality of the life we lead. It can be our greatest ally or our worst adversary.
- A mind that runs amok could steal our inner peace and undermine every productive endeavour.
- Yet, with proper knowledge, training and discipline, it is possible to unleash the mind's infinite potential.
- In The Science of Mind Management, Swami Mukundananda charts the four different aspects of the human mind and lays down a clear path towards mastering it.
- Through witty anecdotes, real-life accounts and stories from the Vedic scriptures, he gently guides readers on the road to winning their inner battle.

WHAT OTHERS SAY:
*This book is by far the best self help book, I have come across.
It has also been launched at a time, when mind management is the need of the hour, with the pandemic and other global crisis enveloping us.*

*Some books has the ability to change the way you think about life, your perspective towards looking the situations or circumstances which you face in your journey of life.
This book is one of them.*

74

THE SECRETS OF THE MILLIONAIRE MIND

AUTHOR: T. HARV EKER

Mastering the Inner Game of Wealth
The missing link between wanting success and achieving it

Amazon (US) star rating: 4.7 ★
Number of Amazon (US) reviews: 3,083
Published: 2005

About the author:

NY Times Bestselling author, T. Harv Eker has helped over 3 million people get closer to their goal of true financial freedom.
Eker is the author of the best-selling books, Secrets of the Millionaire Mind and SpeedWealth.
He has also developed several highly-acclaimed courses such as The Millionaire Mind Intensive, Life Directions, Wizard Training and Train the Trainer.
He is also the producer and trainer of the world-famous Enlightened Warrior Training.
T. Harv Eker is the son of European immigrants who came to North America with only thirty dollars to their name. He grew up in Toronto, but spent most of his adult years in the United States.
harveker.com   IG @t_harveker

more about
THE SECRETS OF THE MILLIONAIRE MIND

- Have you ever wondered why some people seem to get rich easily while others are destined for lives of financial struggle? Is the difference found in their education, intelligence, skills, timing, work habits, contacts, luck, or choice of jobs, businesses, or investments?
- The shocking answer is: none of the above!
- In his groundbreaking Secrets of the Millionaire Mind, T. Harv Eker states, "Give me five minutes, and I can predict your financial future for the rest of your life!" Eker does this by identifying your "money and success blueprint".
- We all have personal money blueprints ingrained in our subconscious minds, and it is these blueprints, more than anything, that will determine our financial lives.
- You can know everything about marketing, sales, negotiations, stocks, real estate, and the world of finance, but if your money blueprint is not set for a high level of success, you will never have a lot of money - and if somehow you do, you will most likely lose it!
- The good news is that now you can actually reset your money blueprint to create natural and automatic success.
- Part I explains how your money blueprint works. Through Eker's rare combination of street smarts, humor, and heart, you will learn how your childhood influences have shaped your financial destiny.
- You will also learn how to identify your own money blueprint and "revise" it not only to create success but, more important, to keep and continually grow it.
- In part II you will be introduced to 17 "Wealth Files", which describe exactly how rich people think and act differently from most poor and middle-class people. Each Wealth File includes action steps for you to practice in the real world in order to dramatically increase your income and accumulate wealth.

WHAT OTHERS SAY:

I've implemented the money management techniques mentioned in the book, and it's been great. The financial balance this book brings was much needed in my life.

75

SECRETS OF SIX-FIGURE WOMEN

AUTHOR: BARBARA HUSON

Surprising Strategies to Up Your Earnings and Change Your Life

Amazon (US) star rating: 4.7 ★
Number of Amazon (US) reviews: 549
Published: 2002

About the author:

Formerly Barbara Stanny, Barbara Huson is the leading authority on Women, Wealth & Power.

She's on a mission to revolutionize women's relationship with money.

As a bestselling author, money & wealth coach, sought after speaker and workshop facilitator, Barbara teaches women to earn the money they deserve, build the wealth they desire, and step fully into their power!

www.Barbara-Huson.com

more about

SECRETS OF SIX-FIGURE WOMEN

- According to the Catalyst.org, in 2018 women's median income was $45,097 annually, which is 81.6% of what men earned. The Gender Wage Gap exists. But that is hardly news.
- But what you may not know is that, quietly and steadily, the number of women making six figures or more is rapidly increasing.
- Currently, over fifteen million women make $100,000 or more, and the number continues to rise at a rate faster than for men. And these women come from every industry - psychologists, dot com founders, consultants, freelance writers, and even part-timers.
- What makes these particular women able to do so well in the workplace? Fueled by curiosity, Barbara Stanny, author of Prince Charming Isn't Coming: How Women Get Smart About Money (Viking Penguin) and Overcoming Underearning (HarperCollins), set out to research this phenomenon.
- What she discovered was that, though the high-earning women she interviewed came from different backgrounds and had had greatly different work experiences, they all had certain characteristics in common.
- Secrets of Six Figure Woman: Surprising Strategies of the Successful High Earners will be a ground breaking book for high earners who want to ensure their wealth, enhance their success, and learn from others who are in the same boat. It will also offer inspiration, guidance, and motivation to those who aspire to make more.

WHAT OTHERS SAY:

This is a must for any woman trying to be free and autonomous.
Every page I read got me more inspired & motivated to keep going.

I'm an Entrepreneur, and while reading the book, I started implementing ideas I had been too scared to try. They are working!

5 stars. Ladies - You NEED this book!
I can't say enough GREAT THINGS about this book! She hit the core of sooo many hidden issues, it changed my entire thought process

76
THE SEVEN HABITS OF HIGHLY EFFECTIVE PEOPLE

AUTHOR: STEPHEN COVEY, UPDATED BY SEAN COVEY

A step-by-step pathway for living with fairness, integrity, honesty, and human dignity.
The #1 Most Influential Business Book of the Twentieth Century

Amazon (US) star rating: 4.8 ★
Number of Amazon (US) reviews: 12,334
First published: 1990

About the authors:
Recognized as one of Time magazine's twenty-five most influential Americans, **Stephen R. Covey** (1932–2012) was an internationally respected leadership authority, family expert, teacher, organizational consultant, and author.
His books have sold more than twenty-five million copies in thirty-eight languages, and The 7 Habits of Highly Effective People was named the #1 Most Influential Business Book of the Twentieth Century.
After receiving an MBA from Harvard and a doctorate degree from Brigham Young University, he became the cofounder and vice chairman of FranklinCovey, a leading global training firm.

Sean Covey, Executive Vice President of Innovation for FranklinCovey Corp., is author of the international bestseller The 7 Habits of Highly Effective Teens, having sold more than 4 million copies and translated into more than twenty languages.
As director of FranklinCovey's education practice, he directed the development project that produced the 4 Disciplines of Execution and teaches transformative strategy and execution to education leaders.
An MBA from Harvard, he is the son of Dr. Stephen R. Covey, author of The 7 Habits of Highly Effective People.

more about
THE SEVEN HABITS OF HIGHLY EFFECTIVE PEOPLE

- One of the most inspiring and impactful books ever written, The 7 Habits of Highly Effective People has captivated readers for nearly three decades.
- It has transformed the lives of presidents and CEOs, educators and parents—millions of people of all ages and occupations.
- The 7 Habits have become famous and are integrated into everyday thinking by millions and millions of people.
- Why? Because they work!
- With Sean Covey's added takeaways on how the habits can be used in our modern age, the wisdom of the 7 Habits will be refreshed for a new generation of leaders. They include:
- Habit 1: Be Proactive
- Habit 2: Begin with the End in Mind
- Habit 3: Put First Things First
- Habit 4: Think Win/Win
- Habit 5: Seek First to Understand, Then to Be Understood
- Habit 6: Synergize
- Habit 7: Sharpen the Saw
- This beloved classic presents a principle-centered approach for solving both personal and professional problems.
- With penetrating insights and practical anecdotes, Stephen R. Covey reveals a step-by-step pathway for living with fairness, integrity, honesty, and human dignity—principles that give us the security to adapt to change and the wisdom and power to take advantage of the opportunities that change creates.

WHAT OTHERS SAY:

"Every so often a book comes along that not only alters the lives of readers but leaves an imprint on the culture itself. The 7 Habits is one of those books." –Daniel Pink, New York Times bestselling author

Next to the Bible, the Most Transformative Book of my Life

77
SHE MEANS BUSINESS

AUTHOR: CARRIE GREEN

Turn Your Ideas into Reality and Become a Wildly Successful Entrepreneur

Amazon (US) star rating: 4.8 ★

Number of Amazon (US) reviews: 1,528

Published: 2017

About the author:

Carrie Green is a female entrepreneur who started her first online business at the age of 20, and within a few years grew her business to global level.

In 2011, after feeling isolated running her business, Carrie started the Female Entrepreneur Association - an online platform with over 750,000 subscribers, which inspires and empowers women from around the world to build successful businesses through videos, classes, and an online community.

Carrie has been recognized as an entrepreneurial "rising star" under the age of 30, and was awarded Entrepreneurs' Champion of the Year in 2014 at the Great British Entrepreneur Awards.

femaleentrepreneurassociation.com   *@iamcarriegreen*

more about
SHE MEANS BUSINESS

- If you're a creative and ambitious female entrepreneur, or are contemplating the entrepreneurial path, this book will provide the honest, realistic, and practical tools you need to follow your heart and bring your vision to life
- With a computer and an Internet connection you can get your ideas, messages, and business out there like never before and create so much success.
- In this book, Carrie Green shows you how.
- She started her first online business at the age of 20—she knows what it's like to be an ambitious and creative woman with big dreams and huge determination . . . but she also knows the challenges of starting and running a business, including the fears, overwhelm, confusion, and blocks that entrepreneurs face.
- Based on her personal, tried-and-tested experience, she offers valuable guidance and powerful exercises to help you:
1. Get clear on your business vision
2. Move past the fears and doubts that can get in the way
3. Understand your audience, so you can truly connect with them
4. Create your brand and build a tribe of raving fans, subscribers, and customers
5. Manage your time, maintain focus, and keep going in the right direction
6. Condition yourself for success.

WHAT OTHERS SAY:

Blown away by this book, it is perhaps my all-time favorite self-help/entrepreneurial book and I am going to read it many times before I am through! I had to get both the audio and paperback versions to use together, and the down to earth insight has me ready to go out and tackle the world.

I had so many light bulb moments and takeways from reading this book. It is a must read for all female entrepreneurs

78
SHOE DOG
AUTHOR: PHIL KNIGHT

A Memoir by the Creator of Nike.
From the early days as an intrepid start-up
and its evolution into one of the world's most
iconic, game-changing, and profitable brands.

Amazon (US) star rating: 4.8 ★

Number of Amazon (US) reviews: 9,502

Published: 2018

About the author:

One of the world's most influential business executives, Phil Knight is the founder of Nike, Inc.

He served as CEO of the company from 1964 to 2004, as board chairman through 2016 (52 years), and he is currently Chairman Emeritus.

Knight ran track at the University of Oregon and created Nike shoes with his former track coach, Bill Bowerman.

In 1964, they each put up $500 to start what would become Nike, then called Blue Ribbon Sports.

He lives in Oregon with his wife, Penny.

more about
SHOE DOG

- In this instant and tenacious New York Times bestseller, Nike founder and board chairman Phil Knight "offers a rare and revealing look at the notoriously media-shy man behind the swoosh" (Booklist, starred review), illuminating his company's early days as an intrepid start-up and its evolution into one of the world's most iconic, game-changing, and profitable brands.
- Fresh out of business school, Phil Knight borrowed fifty dollars from his father and launched a company with one simple mission: import high-quality, low-cost running shoes from Japan.
- Selling the shoes from the trunk of his car in 1963, Knight grossed eight thousand dollars that first year. Today, Nike's annual sales top $30 billion.
- But Knight, the man behind the swoosh, has always been a mystery.
- At twenty-four, Knight decides that rather than work for a big corporation, he will create something all his own, new, dynamic, different.
- He details the many risks he encountered, the crushing setbacks, the ruthless competitors and hostile bankers—as well as his many thrilling triumphs.
- Above all, he recalls the relationships that formed the heart and soul of Nike, with his former track coach, the irascible and charismatic Bill Bowerman, and with his first employees, a ragtag group of misfits and savants who quickly became a band of swoosh-crazed brothers.

WHAT OTHERS SAY:

Bill Gates named Shoe Dog one of his five favorite books of 2016 and called it " a refreshingly honest reminder of what the path to business success really looks like. It's a messy, perilous, and chaotic journey, riddled with mistakes, endless struggles, and sacrifice. Phil Knight opens up in ways few CEOs are willing to do."

*I was a little dubious when I saw so many 5 star reviews
for this book here, but after reading this
I have to say I wholeheartedly agree.*

79
SIDE HUSTLE
AUTHOR: CHRIS GUILLEBEAU

A step by step guide.
From Idea to Income in 27 Days.

Amazon (US) star rating: 4.5 ★
Number of Amazon (US) reviews: 788
Published: 2017

About the author:
During a lifetime of self-employment that included a four-year commitment as a volunteer executive in West Africa, Chris visited every country in the world (193 in total) before his 35th birthday.
Since then he has modeled the proven definition of an entrepreneur: "Someone who will work 24 hours a day for themselves to avoid working one hour a day for someone else."

He is mainly interested in the convergence between highly personal goals and service to others.
You can learn more about that subject in the original Brief Guide to World Domination that was read by more than 100,000 people in 60 countries during the first six months.
His daily podcast, Side Hustle School, is downloaded more than 2 million times a month.

chrisguillebeau.com IG @193countries

more about
SIDE HUSTLE

- For some people, the thought of quitting their day job to pursue the entrepreneurial life is exhilarating. For many others, it's terrifying.
- After all, a stable job that delivers a regular paycheck is a blessing.
- And not everyone has the means or the desire to take on the risks and responsibilities of working for themselves.
- But what if we could quickly and easily create an additional stream of income without giving up the security of a full-time job?
- Enter the side hustle.
- Designed for the busy and impatient, this detailed roadmap will show you how to select, launch, refine, and make money from your side hustle in under a month. You'll learn how to:
1. Brainstorm, borrow, and steal to build an arsenal of great side hustle ideas
2. Apply "Tinder for Side Hustle" logic to pick the best idea at any time
3. Learn, gather, or create everything you need to launch; then set up a real life way to get paid
4. Start raking in the money by channeling your inner Girl Scout
5. Master the art of deals, discounts, and special offers
6. Raise your game: improve, expand, or make more money off your hustle
- A side hustle is more than just another stream of income, it's also the new job security. When you receive paychecks from different sources, it allows you to take more chances in your "regular" career.
- More income means more options. More options equals freedom.

WHAT OTHERS SAY
Did it work for me? Yep. I'm already earning extra money on the side.

Thinking of launching a side hustle?
You'd be a fool not to read this book!

This book breaks down selecting and building a side hustle into simple bite-sized daily chunks.

80
THE SLIGHT EDGE
AUTHOR: JEFF OLSON

Turning Simple Disciplines into Massive Success and Happiness

Amazon (US) star rating: 4.7 ★
Number of Amazon (US) reviews: 3,259
First published: 2013

About the author:
Jeff Olson has built multimillion-dollar sales and marketing organizations, hosted seminars in every major city in the U.S. and has produced over 900 television programs with such personal development legends as Les Brown, Jim Rohn and Brian Tracy.
Over the past twenty years, Jeff has helped hundreds of thousands of individuals achieve better levels of financial freedom and personal excellence.
Fueled by his passion for making the world a better place, Jeff devotes his time to serving on the board of the Neora Ripple Foundation and has helped raise over $5 million for Big Brothers Big Sisters (BBBS) and World Vision International.
He has also committed resources to the Success Foundation, founded Live Happy magazine, and supported the International Positive Education Network.
Jeff has addressed the United Nations on the topic of global happiness and has been inducted into the Happiness Hall of Fame.
neora.com

more about
THE SLIGHT EDGE

- The Slight Edge is a way of thinking, a way of processing information that enables you to make the daily choices that will lead you to the success and happiness you desire.
- Learn why some people make dream after dream come true, while others just continue dreaming and spend their lives building dreams for someone else.
- It's not just another self-help motivation tool of methods you must learn in order to travel the path to success.
- It shows you how to create powerful results from the simple daily activities of your life, by using tools that are already within you.
- In this 8th anniversary edition you'll read not only the life-changing concepts of the original book, but also learn what author Jeff Olson discovered as he continued along the slight edge path: the Secret to Happiness and the Ripple Effect.
- This edition of The Slight Edge isn't just the story, but also how the story continues to create life-altering dynamics; how a way of thinking, a way of processing information, can impact daily choices that will lead to the success and happiness you desire.
- The Slight Edge is the key that will make all the other how-to books and self-help information that you read, actually work

WHAT OTHERS SAY

As a result of reading this book, I committed to reading 10 pages of a good book every day. From there, other little changes started flowing.

Now, 3 years later, I've read (or listened to) over 40 great books, transformed the relationships I have with my friends and family, and has even inspired me to create my own Rise Up movement to pay it forward.

I've read the paperback so many times that it's held together with paperclips and a rubber band.

81
START WITH WHY

AUTHOR: SIMON SINEK

How Great Leaders Inspire Everyone to Take Action

Amazon (US) star rating: 4.6 ★
Number of Amazon (US) reviews: 9,845
Published: 2011

About the author:

Simon Sinek, also the bestselling author of LEADERS EAT LAST and TOGETHER IS BETTER, is an optimist who believes in a brighter future for humanity.

He teaches leaders and organizations how to inspire people and has presented his ideas around the world, from small startups to Fortune 50 corporations, from Hollywood to Congress to the Pentagon.

His TED Talk based on START WITH WHY is the third most popular TED video of all time.

StartWithWhy.com   *IG* @simonsinek

more about
START WITH WHY

- In 2009, Simon Sinek started a movement to help people become more inspired, and in turn inspire their colleagues and customers.
- Since then, millions have been touched by the power of his ideas, including more than 28 million who've watched his TED Talk based on START WITH WHY -- the third most popular TED video of all time.
- Sinek starts with a fundamental question:
- Why are some people and organizations more innovative, more influential, and more profitable than others?
- Why do some command greater loyalty from customers and employees alike?
- Even among the successful, why are so few able to repeat their success over and over?
- People like Martin Luther King Jr., Steve Jobs, and the Wright Brothers had little in common, but they all started with WHY.
- They realized that people won't truly buy into a product, service, movement, or idea until they understand the WHY behind it.
- START WITH WHY shows that the leaders who've had the greatest influence in the world all think, act, and communicate the same way -- and it's the opposite of what everyone else does.
- Sinek calls this powerful idea The Golden Circle, and it provides a framework upon which organizations can be built, movements can be led, and people can be inspired.
- And it all starts with WHY.

WHAT OTHERS SAY

"Each story will force you to see things from an entirely different perspective. A perspective that is nothing short of the truth."
-MOKHTAR LAMANI, former ambassador, special envoy to Iraq

While the majority of this book is about companies and the people who lead them, it is completely relatable to your personal life outside of work

82
(BUILDING A) STORYBRAND

AUTHOR: DONALD MILLER

Use the 7 Elements of Great Storytelling to Build your Business. Clarify Your Message So Customers Will Listen

Amazon (US) star rating: 4.7 ★
Number of Amazon (US) reviews: 2,570
Published: 2017

About the author:

Donald Miller is the CEO of StoryBrand, the cohost of the Building a StoryBrand Podcast, and the author of several books Every year helps more than 3,000 business leaders clarify their brand message. Don is widely considered one of the most entertaining and informative speakers in the world. His audiences are challenged to lean into their own story, creatively develop and execute the story of their team, and understand the story of their customers so they can serve them with passion. Don's thoughts on story have deeply influenced leaders and teams for Pantene, Chick-fil-A, Steelcase, Intel, Prime Lending, Zaxby's, and thousands more. Don lives in Nashville, Tennessee, with his wife, Betsy, and their chocolate lab, Lucy.

*storybrand.com   IG @storybrand_*

more about
BUILDING A STORYBRAND

- Donald Miller uses the seven universal elements of powerful stories to teach listeners how to dramatically improve how they connect with customers and grow their businesses.
- His StoryBrand process is a proven solution to the struggle business leaders face when talking about their businesses.
- This revolutionary method for connecting with customers provides listeners with the ultimate competitive advantage, revealing the secret for helping their customers understand the compelling benefits of using their products, ideas, or services.
- Building a StoryBrand does this by teaching listeners the seven universal story points all humans respond to, the real reason customers make purchases, how to simplify a brand message so people understand it, and how to create the most effective messaging for websites, brochures, and social media.
- Whether you are the marketing director of a multibillion-dollar company, the owner of a small business, a politician running for office, or the lead singer of a rock band, Building a StoryBrand will forever transform the way you talk about who you are, what you do, and the unique value you bring to your customers.

WHAT OTHERS SAY

Great whether you're a copywriting pro or a complete novice.

Your audience will start paying attention if you do it this way, Donald Miller makes it easy. I've read this twice through. I have tabs (7 of them) to go back to each step to re-visit details.

We see it work every day My team has followed Donald Miller and the StoryBrand framework for a couple years now. We've been applying it to our clients and watching them grow.

83
THE SUBTLE ART OF NOT GIVING A F*CK

AUTHOR: MARK MANSON

A Counterintuitive Approach to Living a Good Life

Amazon (US) star rating: 4.6 ★
Number of Amazon (US) reviews: 30,565
Published: 2016

About the author:

Mark Manson is the #1 New York Times Bestselling author of Everything is F*cked: A Book About Hope and The Subtle Art of Not Giving a F*ck: A Counterintuitive Approach to Living a Good Life, the mega-bestseller that reached #1 in fourteen different countries.
Mark's books have been translated into more than 50 languages and have sold over 12 million copies worldwide.
Mark runs one of the largest personal growth websites in the world, MarkManson.net, a blog with more than two million monthly readers and half a million subscribers.
His writing is often described as 'self-help for people who hate self-help' — a no-BS brand of life advice and cultural commentary that has struck a chord with people around the globe.
His writing has appeared in The New York Times, Wall Street Journal, TIME Magazine, Forbes, Vice, CNN, and Vox, among many others.
He currently lives in New York City.
MarkManson.net IG @markmanson

more about
THE SUBTLE ART OF NOT GIVING A F*CK

- In this generation-defining self-help guide, a superstar blogger cuts through the crap to show us how to stop trying to be "positive" all the time so that we can truly become better, happier people.
- For decades, we've been told that positive thinking is the key to a happy, rich life. "F**k positivity," Mark Manson says. "Let's be honest, shit is f**ked and we have to live with it."
- The Subtle Art of Not Giving a F**k is his antidote to the coddling, let's-all-feel-good mindset that has infected modern society and spoiled a generation, rewarding them with gold medals just for showing up.
- Manson makes the argument, backed both by academic research and well-timed poop jokes, that improving our lives hinges not on our ability to turn lemons into lemonade, but on learning to stomach lemons better.
- Once we embrace our fears, faults, and uncertainties, once we stop running and avoiding and start confronting painful truths, we can begin to find the courage, perseverance, honesty, responsibility, curiosity, and forgiveness we seek.
- There are only so many things we can give a f**k about so we need to figure out which ones really matter, Manson makes clear.
- While money is nice, caring about what you do with your life is better, because true wealth is about experience.
- A much-needed grab-you-by-the-shoulders-and-look-you-in-the-eye moment of real-talk, filled with entertaining stories and profane, ruthless humor, The Subtle Art of Not Giving a F**k is a refreshing slap for a generation to help them lead contented, grounded lives.

WHAT OTHERS SAY:

"Resilience, happiness and freedom come from knowing what to care about--and most importantly, what not to care about.
Ryan Holiday, New York Times bestselling author

This book hits you like a much-needed slap in the face from your best friend: hilarious, vulgar, and immensely thought-provoking.

84
THE SUCCESS PRINCIPLES

AUTHORS: JACK CANFIELD & JANET SWITZER

How to Get from Where You Are to Where You Want to Be

Amazon (US) star rating: 4.8 ★
Number of Amazon (US) reviews: 2,908
First published: 2004

About the authors:

Jack Canfield, America's #1 Success Coach, is the cocreator of the Chicken Soup for the Soul® series, which includes forty New York Times bestsellers, and coauthor with Gay Hendricks of You've GOT to Read This Book!An internationally renowned corporate trainer, keynote speaker, and popular radio and TV talk show guest, he lives in Santa Barbara, California.

Janet Switzer is the New York Times bestselling coauthor of The Success Principles with Jack Canfield, co-creator of the phenomenal Chicken Soup for the Soul franchise. She has also developed successful campaigns in media, direct mail, and specialty marketing for many of the most renowned celebrity entrepreneurs in the world.

jackcanfield.com   *@jackcanfield_official*

more about
THE SUCCESS PRINCIPLES

- In celebration of its 10th anniversary, a revised and updated edition of Jack Canfield's classic bestseller with a brand new foreword and an afterword for succeeding in the digital age.
- Since its publication a decade ago, Jack Canfield's practical and inspiring guide has helped thousands of people transform themselves for success.
- Now, he has revised and updated his essential guidebook to reflect our changing times.
- In The Success Principles, the cocreator of the phenomenal bestselling Chicken Soup for the Soul series, helps you get from where you are to where you want to be, teaching you how to increase your confidence, tackle daily challenges, live with passion and purpose, and realize all your ambitions.
- Filled with memorable and inspiring stories of CEO's, world-class athletes, celebrities, and everyday people, it spells out the 64 timeless principles used by successful men and women throughout history—proven principles and strategies that can be adapted for your own life, whether you want to be the best salesperson in your company, become a leading architect, score top grades in school, lose weight, buy your dream home, make millions, or just get back in the job market.
- Taken together and practiced every day, these principles will change your life beyond your wildest dreams.

WHAT OTHERS SAY

This book is an absolute must read for anyone who wishes to achieve a more successful and happier life. Jack Canfield reveals the specific requirements, methods and principles for breaking through and achieving success in life, work, health and love.

Five stars. This book changed my life!

85
TALKING TO STRANGERS

AUTHOR: MALCOLM GLADWELL

What We Should Know about the People We Don't Know

Amazon (US) star rating: 4.5 ★
Number of Amazon (US) reviews: 7,019
Published: 2019

About the author:

Malcolm Gladwell is the author of five New York Times bestsellers — The Tipping Point, Blink,Outliers, What the Dog Saw, and David and Goliath.
He is also the co-founder of Pushkin Industries, an audio content company that produces the podcasts Revisionist History, which reconsiders things both overlooked and misunderstood, and Broken Record, where he, Rick Rubin, and Bruce Headlam interview musicians across a wide range of genres.
Gladwell has been included in the TIME 100 Most Influential People list and touted as one of Foreign Policy's Top Global Thinkers.

www.gladwellbooks.com   IG @malcolmgladwell

more about
TALKING TO STRANGERS

- A Best Book of the Year: The Financial Times, Bloomberg, Chicago Tribune, and Detroit Free Pres
- Malcolm Gladwell offers a powerful examination of our interactions with strangers -- and why they often go wrong.
- How did Fidel Castro fool the CIA for a generation? Why did Neville Chamberlain think he could trust Adolf Hitler? Why are campus sexual assaults on the rise? Do television sitcoms teach us about the way we relate to each other that isn't true?
- While tackling these questions, Malcolm Gladwell was not solely writing a book for the page. He was also producing for the ear. In the audiobook version of Talking to Strangers, you'll hear the voices of people he interviewed--scientists, criminologists, military psychologists. Court transcripts are brought to life with re-enactments.
- You actually hear the contentious arrest of Sandra Bland by the side of the road in Texas. As Gladwell revisits the deceptions of Bernie Madoff, the trial of Amanda Knox, and the suicide of Sylvia Plath, you hear directly from many of the players in these real-life tragedies. There's even a theme song - Janelle Monae's "Hell You Talmbout."
- Something is very wrong, Gladwell argues, with the tools and strategies we use to make sense of people we don't know. And because we don't know how to talk to strangers, we are inviting conflict and misunderstanding in ways that have a profound effect on our lives and our world.

WHAT OTHERS SAY

"Talking to Strangers is a must-read...I love this book... Reading it will actually change not just how you see strangers, but how you look at yourself, the news--the world...Reading this book changed me."—Oprah Winfrey, O, The Oprah Magazine
It is a must read for anybody who needs to make snap judgements about people's character and behavior.

86
THINK AND GROW RICH

AUTHOR: NAPOLEON HILL
UPDATED BY ARTHUR R. PELL, PH.D

"The Granddaddy of All
Motivational Literature."
It was the first book to boldly ask,
"What makes a winner?"
Updated for the 21st century.

Amazon (US) star rating: 4.7 ★

Number of Amazon (US) reviews: 30,164

First published: 1937

About the author:
Napoleon Hill was born in 1883 in Virginia and died in 1970 after a long and successful career as a lecturer, an author, and as a consultant to business leaders.

Think and Grow Rich is the all-time bestseller in its field, having sold 15 million copies worldwide, and sets the standard for today's motivational thinking.

more about
THINK AND GROW RICH

- It was the first book to boldly ask, "What makes a winner?"
- The man who asked and listened for the answer, Napoleon Hill, is now counted in the top ranks of the world's winners himself.
- The most famous of all teachers of success spent "a fortune and the better part of a lifetime of effort" to produce the "Law of Success" philosophy that forms the basis of his books and that is so powerfully summarized in this one.
- In the original Think and Grow Rich, published in 1937, Hill draws on stories of Andrew Carnegie, Thomas Edison, Henry Ford, and other millionaires to illustrate his principles.
- In the updated version, Arthur R. Pell, Ph.D., a nationally known author, lecturer, and consultant in human resources management and an expert in applying Hill's thought, deftly interweaves anecdotes of how contemporary millionaires and billionaires, such as Bill Gates, Mary Kay Ash, Dave Thomas, and Sir John Templeton, achieved their wealth.
- Outmoded terminology and examples are faithfully refreshed to preclude stumbling blocks to a new generation of readers.

WHAT OTHERS SAY:
If I could I would have given 10 stars!
Yes this book will change your life.

Extremely helpful in handlling CRITICISM and how to move on.....

In your journey for success, and I've read over 150 books on business and personal development, this is the godfather.

I chose to read this book because I have met several people who have read it and they say, it's a game changer.
This book is filled with confirmation , spiritual truth , and wisdom beyond your imagination.

87
THINKING, FAST AND SLOW

AUTHOR: DANIEL KAHNEMAN

A groundbreaking tour of the mind, explaining the two systems that drive the way we think.

Amazon (US) star rating: 4.6 ★
Number of Amazon (US) reviews: 12,446
Published: 2013

About the author:
Daniel Kahneman is an Israeli psychologist and economist notable for his work on the psychology of judgment and decision-making, as well as behavioral economics.

He has been the recipient of many awards, among them the Distinguished Scientific Contribution Award of the American Psychological Association (1982) and the Grawemeyer Prize (2002), both jointly with Amos Tversky, the Warren Medal of the Society of Experimental Psychologists (1995), the Hilgard Award for Career Contributions to General Psychology (1995), the Nobel Prize in Economic Sciences (2002), and the Lifetime Contribution Award of the American Psychological Association (2007).

more about
THINKING, FAST AND SLOW

- In his mega bestseller, Daniel Kahneman takes us on a groundbreaking tour of the mind and explains the two systems that drive the way we think.
- System 1 is fast, intuitive, and emotional;
- System 2 is slower, more deliberative, and more logical.
- The impact of overconfidence on corporate strategies, the difficulties of predicting what will make us happy in the future, the profound effect of cognitive biases on everything from playing the stock market to planning our next vacation—each of these can be understood only by knowing how the two systems shape our judgments and decisions.
- Engaging the reader in a lively conversation about how we think, he reveals where we can and cannot trust our intuitions and how we can tap into the benefits of slow thinking.
- He offers practical and enlightening insights into how choices are made in both our business and our personal lives—and how we can use different techniques to guard against the mental glitches that often get us into trouble.
- Topping bestseller lists for almost ten years, Thinking, Fast and Slow is a contemporary classic, an essential book that has changed the lives of millions of readers.

WHAT OTHERS SAY

To anyone with the slightest interest in the workings of his own mind, it is so rich and fascinating that any summary would seem absurd."
—Michael Lewis, Vanity Fair

Understand How You Can Be Manipulated on Social Media
Certainly the most thought provoking book I've read in a long time.

It's a must read for everyone who believes in improving the habits relating to your sub-conscious thinking.

88
THINK LIKE A MONK

AUTHOR: JAY SHETTY

Train Your Mind for Peace and Purpose Every Day

Amazon (US) star rating: 4.9 ★

Number of Amazon (US) reviews: 7,410

Published: 2020

About the author:

Jay Shetty is a New York Times best-selling author, storyteller, podcaster, and former monk.

He is on a mission to share the timeless wisdom of the world in an accessible, relevant, and practical way.

Shetty has created over 400 viral videos and hosts the #1 Health and Wellness podcast in the world, On Purpose.

Today Jay Shetty is considered one of the most powerful people in the world with a vast social media reach, amassing 38.5M+ million followers and 8 billion views for his "Making Wisdom Go Viral" videos.

JayShetty.me   IG @jayshetty

more about
THINK LIKE A MONK

- Shetty grew up in a family where you could become one of three things—a doctor, a lawyer, or a failure. His family was convinced he had chosen option three: instead of attending his college graduation ceremony, he headed to India to become a monk, to meditate every day for four to eight hours, and devote his life to helping others.
- After three years, one of his teachers told him that he would have more impact on the world if he left the monk's path to share his experience and wisdom with others. Heavily in debt, and with no recognizable skills on his résumé, he moved back home in north London with his parents.
- Shetty reconnected with old school friends—many working for some of the world's largest corporations—who were experiencing tremendous stress, pressure, and unhappiness, and they invited Shetty to coach them on well-being, purpose, and mindfulness.
- Since then, Shetty has become one of the world's most popular influencers.
- Drawing on ancient wisdom and his own rich experiences in the ashram, Think Like a Monk reveals how to overcome negative thoughts and habits to access the calm and purpose that lie within all of us.
- The lessons monks learn are profound but often abstract.
- In Think Like a Monk, Jay transforms them into simple advice and exercises we can all apply to reduce stress, sharpen focus, improve relationships, identify our hidden abilities, increase self-discipline, and give the gifts we find in ourselves to the world. Jay proves that everyone can—and should—think like a monk.

WHAT OTHERS SAY

"Jay Shetty shows you step by step how to build your power by shifting your focus from self-image to self-esteem. This book frees you from the hypnosis of social conditioning and helps you become the architect of your own life."
—Deepak Chopra, MD., New York Times bestselling author of The Seven Spiritual Laws of Success

"Jay Shetty has a rare gift for tapping into the world's timeless wisdom and making it timely by infusing everyday moments with meaning and grace. He's already shared glimmers of that wisdom with millions on social media, but here he gathers it all into one life-changing volume. Read this book to open your mind, lift your heart, redefine success and connect with your deeper purpose."
—Arianna Huffington, Founder of The Huffington Post, Founder and CEO of Thrive Global, and New York Times bestselling author

89
THE TIPPING POINT
AUTHOR: MALCOLM GLADWELL

How Little Things Can Make a Big Difference. Exploring the science behind viral trends in business, marketing, and human behavior.

Amazon (US) star rating: 4.5 ★

Number of Amazon (US) reviews: 3,667

Published: 2002

About the author:

Malcolm Gladwell is the author of five New York Times bestsellers – The Tipping Point, Blink, Outliers, What the Dog Saw, and David and Goliath.

He is also the co-founder of Pushkin Industries, an audio content company that produces the podcasts Revisionist History, which reconsiders things both overlooked and misunderstood, and Broken Record, where he, Rick Rubin, and Bruce Headlam interview musicians across a wide range of genres.

Gladwell has been included in the TIME 100 Most Influential People list and touted as one of Foreign Policy's Top Global Thinkers.

www.gladwellbooks.com   IG @malcolmgladwell

more about
THE TIPPING POINT

- Discover Malcolm Gladwell's breakthrough debut and explore the science behind viral trends in business, marketing, and human behavior.
- The tipping point is that magic moment when an idea, trend, or social behavior crosses a threshold, tips, and spreads like wildfire.
- Just as a single sick person can start an epidemic of the flu, so too can a small but precisely targeted push cause a fashion trend, the popularity of a new product, or a drop in the crime rate.
- This widely acclaimed bestseller, in which Malcolm Gladwell explores and brilliantly illuminates the tipping point phenomenon, is already changing the way people throughout the world think about selling products and disseminating ideas.

WHAT OTHERS SAY:

Malcolm Gladwell Explains the Secret to Enable you to Launch a Product Successfully.

I consider this the best marketing book of all time. It was written before e-commerce, but has become even more relevant as e-commerce has advanced. It also provides some useful ideas for doing sales in general

This book is awesome because it sharpens your mind eye to see the things that can cause an epidemic or start the next fad in popular culture. This book is a must read for persons who desire to make big impact on this tightly connected world.

90
TOOLS OF TITANS
AUTHOR: TIM FERRISS

The Tactics, Routines, and Habits of Billionaires, Icons, and World-Class Performers

Amazon (US) star rating: 4.6 ★
Number of Amazon (US) reviews: 4,655
Published: 2016

About the author:

Tim Ferriss is a serial entrepreneur, #1 New York Times bestselling author, and angel investor/advisor (Facebook, Twitter, Evernote, Uber, and 20+ more).

Best known for his rapid-learning techniques, Tim's books -- The 4-Hour Workweek, The 4-Hour Body, and The 4-Hour Chef -- have been published in 30+ languages. The 4-Hour Workweek has spent seven years on The New York Times bestseller list.

Tim has been featured by more than 100 media outlets including The New York Times, The Economist, TIME, Forbes, Fortune, Outside, NBC, CBS, ABC, Fox and CNN.

He has guest lectured in entrepreneurship at Princeton University since 2003.

His popular blog www has 1M+ monthly readers, and his Twitter account @tferriss was selected by Mashable as one of only five "Must-Follow" accounts for entrepreneurs.

Tim's primetime TV show, The Tim Ferriss Experiment (www.upwave.com/tfx), teaches rapid-learning techniques for helping viewers to produce seemingly superhuman results in minimum time.

fourhourblog.com   IG @timferriss

more about
TOOLS OF TITANS

- For the last two years, I've interviewed more than 200 world-class performers for my podcast, The Tim Ferriss Show. The guests range from super celebs (Jamie Foxx, Arnold Schwarzenegger, etc.) and athletes (icons of powerlifting, gymnastics, surfing, etc.) to legendary Special Operations commanders and black-market biochemists.
- For most of my guests, it's the first time they've agreed to a two-to-three-hour interview.
- This unusual depth has helped make The Tim Ferriss Show the first business/interview podcast to pass 100 million downloads.
- What makes the show different is a relentless focus on actionable details. This is reflected in the questions. For example: What do these people do in the first 60 minutes of each morning? What do their workout routines look like, and why? What books have they gifted most to other people? What are the biggest wastes of time for novices in their field? What supplements do they take on a daily basis?
- I view myself as an experimenter. If I can't test and replicate results in the messy reality of everyday life, I'm not interested.
- Everything has been vetted, explored, and applied to my own life in some fashion. I've used dozens of the tactics and philosophies in high-stakes negotiations, high-risk environments, or large business dealings.
- The lessons have made me millions of dollars and saved me years of wasted effort and frustration.
- "I created this book, my ultimate notebook of high-leverage tools, for myself. It's changed my life, and I hope the same for you.

WHAT OTHERS SAY
Had I had this book from the start of my business, I would have avoided half the mistakes and saved a lot of time.

Must read if you have the guts to dream big and follow through

91
TRAFFIC SECRETS
AUTHOR: RUSSELL BRUNSON

The Underground Playbook for Filling Your Websites and Funnels with Your Dream Customers

Amazon (US) star rating: 4.8 ★

Number of Amazon (US) reviews: 588

Published: 2020

About the author: Russell Brunson is a serial entrepreneur who started his first online company while he was wrestling at Boise State University.

Within a year of graduating he had sold over a million dollars worth of his own products and services from his basement!
For over 10 years now Russell has been starting and scaling companies online.

Russell has built a following of over a million entrepreneurs, sold hundreds of thousands of copies of his best selling books, popularized the concept of sales funnels, and co-founded a software company called ClickFunnelsthat helps tens of thousands of entrepreneurs quickly get their message out to the marketplace.

russellbrunson.com

more about
TRAFFIC SECRETS

- The biggest problem that most entrepreneurs have isn't creating an amazing product or service; it's getting their future customers to discover that they even exist.
- Every year, tens of thousands of businesses start and fail because the entrepreneurs don't understand this one essential skill: the art and science of getting traffic (or people) to find you. That is a tragedy.
- Traffic Secrets was written to help you get your message out to the world about your products and services. I strongly believe that entrepreneurs are the only people on earth who can actually change the world. It won't happen in government, and I don't think it will happen in schools.
- It'll happen because of entrepreneurs like you, who are crazy enough to build products and services that will actually change the world. It'll happen because we are crazy enough to risk everything to try and make that dream become a reality.
- To all the entrepreneurs who fail in their first year of business, what a tragedy it is when the one thing they risked everything for never fully gets to see the light of day.
- Understanding exactly WHO your dream customer is, discovering where they're congregating, and throwing out the hooks that will grab their attention to pull them into your funnels (where you can tell them a story and make them an offer) is the strategy. That's the big secret.
- Traffic is just people. This book will help you find YOUR people, so you can focus on changing their world with the products and services that you sell.

WHAT OTHERS SAY:

For me, Russell is just next to Seth Godin and Guy Kawasaki, with the exception the Russell explain the evergreen step by step that any other author does.

My faith in online visibility is alive thanks to Traffic Secrets and Russell.

Five Stars. For Smart Entrepreneurs Wanting More Leads & Sales From EVERGREEN Frameworks!

92
THE ULTIMATE SALES MACHINE

AUTHOR: CHET HOLMES (1957-2012)

Turbocharge Your Business with Relentless Focus on 12 Key Strategies

Amazon (US) star rating: 4.6 ★

Number of Amazon (US) reviews: 676

Published: 2008

About the author:

Chet Holmes was an acclaimed corporate trainer, strategic mastermind, business growth expert, and lecturer.

Considered one of the world's foremost marketing and sales experts, he has designed more than 500 advertising campaigns and had 60 of the Fortune 500 as clients.

The realization of Chet's discoveries came to full fruition while running nine divisions of a company for Charlie Munger (on the Forbes "Billionaires" list, partner of Warren Buffett).

Chet Holmes doubled the sales volume of each division, most within only 12 to 15 months, continuing strategic growth in several divisions and again doubling sales for several years consecutively.

Charlie has called Chet, "America's greatest sales and marketing executive.

He focussed on 12 competencies which became the foundation for more than 65 training products now selling in 23 countries.

more about
THE ULTIMATE SALES MACHINE

- The Ultimate Sales Machine will blow away both the competition and their own expectations.
- Chet's advice starts with one simple concept: focus!
- Instead of trying to master four thousand strategies to improve your business, zero in on the few essential skill areas that make the big difference.
- The Ultimate Sales Machine shows you how to tune up and soup up virtually every part of your business by spending just an hour per week on each impact area you want to improve? Sales, marketing, management, and more.

WHAT OTHERS SAY:

This is by far the best sales book I have ever read, and I have read hundreds.?
A. Harrison Barnes, CEO, Juriscape

Although this book can be considered 'out of date' in some ways, you can still adapt the information to online businesses. I found this so valuable that I couldn't close my Kindle App until I'd finished reading most of it. Some gems that I've already taken on board and benefited from, big time.
If you run a business / are involved in selling, you must read this.

The BEST and Only Business book you need to read! Chet is a Genius - no questions asked. The book covers everything you need to know to turn your company into a sales machine.
I had so many "Eureka" moments reading this book it was crazy and I have been in business quite a long time.

93
UNSHAKEABLE
AUTHORS: TONY ROBBINS & PETER MALLOUK

How to put together a simple, actionable plan that can deliver true financial freedom

Amazon (US) star rating: 4.6 ★

Number of Amazon (US) reviews: 2,679

Published: 2017

About the authors:

Tony Robbins has coached more than fifty million people from 100 countries. He is is a life and business strategist, a philanthropist and #1 New York Times bestselling author. He lives in Palm Beach, Florida. tonyrobbins.com

Peter Mallouk has twice been named to the Worth list of the 100 Most Powerful Individuals in the world of Global Finance.

He has also been named the #1 Financial Advisor in America by Barron's (three consecutive years from 2013-2015) and his firm, Creative Planning, has been ranked the #1 Independent Wealth Management firm in the US by CNBC for two consecutive years.

creativeplanning.com

more about
UNSHAKEABLE

- In this book, Tony teams up with Peter Mallouk, the only man in history to be ranked the #1 financial advisor in the US for three consecutive years by Barron's.
- Together they reveal how to become unshakeable—someone who can not only maintain true peace of mind in a world of immense uncertainty, economic volatility, and unprecedented change, but who can profit from the fear that immobilizes so many.
- After interviewing 50 of the world's greatest financial minds his #1 New York Times bestseller Money: Master the Game, Tony Robbins returns with a step-by-step playbook, helping you to transform your financial life & accelerate your path to financial freedom.
- No matter your salary, your stage of life, or when you started, this book will provide the tools to help you achieve your financial goals more rapidly than you ever thought possible. You'll learn:
1.-How to put together a simple, actionable plan that can deliver true financial freedom.
2.-Strategies from the world's top investors on how to protect yourself and your family and maximize profit from the inevitable crashes and corrections to come.
3.-How a few simple steps can add a decade or more of additional retirement income by discovering what your 401(k) provider doesn't want you to know.
4.-The core four principles that most of the world's greatest financial minds utilize so that you can maximize upside and minimize downside.
5.-The fastest way to put money back in your pocket: uncover the hidden fees and half truths of Wall Street—how the biggest firms keep you overpaying for underperformance.

WHAT OTHERS SAY:

One of those books, which before I finished them, realized that they changed something significant about my life.

94
UNTAMED

AUTHOR: GLENNON DOYLE

An intimate memoir and a galvanizing wake-up call. How to be Brave.

Amazon (US) star rating: 4.7 ★
Number of Amazon (US) reviews: 20,441
Published: 2020

About the author:
Glennon Doyle is the author of the #1 New York Times bestseller Love Warrior, an Oprah's Book Club selection, as well as the New York Times bestseller Carry On, Warrior.

An activist, speaker, and thought leader, she is also the founder and president of Together Rising, an all-women led nonprofit organization that has revolutionized grassroots philanthropy—raising over $20 million for women, families, and children in crisis, with a most frequent donation of just $25.

Glennon was named among OWN Network's SuperSoul 100 inaugural group as one of 100 "awakened leaders who are using their voices and talent to elevate humanity."
She lives in Florida with her wife and three children.

momastery.com   IG *@glennondoyle*

more about UNTAMED

- In her most revealing and powerful memoir yet, the activist, speaker, bestselling author, and "patron saint of female empowerment" explores the joy and peace we discover when we stop striving to meet others' expectations and start trusting the voice deep within.
- There is a voice of longing inside each woman.
- We strive so mightily to be good: good partners, daughters, mothers, employees, and friends.
- We hope all this striving will make us feel alive.
- Instead, it leaves us feeling weary, stuck, overwhelmed, and underwhelmed. We look at our lives and wonder: Wasn't it all supposed to be more beautiful than this? We quickly silence that question, telling ourselves to be grateful, hiding our discontent—even from ourselves.
- For many years, Glennon Doyle denied her own discontent. Then, while speaking at a conference, she looked at a woman across the room and fell instantly in love.
- Three words flooded her mind: There She Is. At first, Glennon assumed these words came to her from on high. But she soon realized they had come to her from within.
- This was her own voice—the one she had buried beneath decades of numbing addictions, cultural conditioning, and institutional allegiances. Glennon decided to quit abandoning herself and to instead abandon the world's expectations of her. She quit being good so she could be free. She quit pleasing and started living.
- Untamed is both an intimate memoir and a galvanizing wake-up call. It is the story of how one woman learned that a responsible mother is not one who slowly dies for her children, but one who shows them how to fully live.

WHAT OTHERS SAY:

"Untamed will liberate women—emotionally, spiritually, & physically.
It is phenomenal."
Elizabeth Gilbert, author of City of Girls and Eat Pray Love

95
WHAT GOT YOU HERE WON'T GET YOU THERE

AUTHORS: MARSHALL GOLDSMITH & MARK REITER

How Successful People Become Even More Successful

Amazon (US) star rating: 4.6 ★
Number of Amazon (US) reviews: 1,801
Published: 2007

About the author:

Marshall Goldsmith is one of the world's most accomplished and in-demand executive coaches.

With a client list that is a who's who of the highest level global CEOs, he is very selective in choosing clients. He currently has a waiting list of six months for any potential new clients.

Marshall's coaching process is unique. He only gets paid after his clients get better! "Better" is not defined by Marshall or by his individual clients.
"Better" means measurable positive change in pre-selected leadership behaviors as determined by pre-selected key stakeholders.

He is a new member of the Thinkers 50 Hall of Fame, the only two-time Thinkers 50 #1 Leadership Thinker in the World, ranked as the World's #1 Executive Coach and Top Ten Business Thinker for 8 years.

He is the author or editor of 41 books, which have sold over 2.5 million copies, been translated into 32 languages and become listed bestsellers in 12 countries.

marshallgoldsmith.com

more about

WHAT GOT YOU HERE
WON'T GET YOU THERE

- America's most sought-after executive coach shows how to climb the last few rungs of the ladder.
- The corporate world is filled with executives, men and women who have worked hard for years to reach the upper levels of management.
- They're intelligent, skilled, and even charismatic.
- But only a handful of them will ever reach the pinnacle - and as executive coach Marshall Goldsmith shows in this book, subtle nuances make all the difference.
- These are small "transactional flaws" performed by one person against another (as simple as not saying thank you enough), which lead to negative perceptions that can hold any executive back.
- Using Goldsmith's straightforward, jargon-free advice, it's amazingly easy behavior to change.

WHAT OTHERS SAY:

These are words and processes anyone will benefit from, whether wannabe manager or senior executive.
Barbara Jacobs, Booklist

Mr. Goldsmith writes in a very conversational style. He has a wealth of experience in working with some of the most successful people in the world and has brought his experiences together and shares a number of success stories.

Excellent book! This had helped to reduce my mind chatter so much and has helped me be more direct with people and also realize the importance of how to carry yourself with people.

96
WHAT IF IT DOES WORK OUT ?
AUTHOR: SUSIE MOORE

How a Side Hustle Can Change Your Life

Amazon (US) star rating: 4.6 ★
Number of Amazon (US) reviews: 149
Published: 2017

About the author:
Susie Moore not only talks the talk, she walks the walk.

After leaving her highly profitable yet ultimately unsatisfying career as a Fortune 500 sales director, Susie has become a successful business and life coach, advising high-growth startups in Silicon Valley and New York City, all of which sold, the most recent for $405 million.

With years of experience on the front-lines of the side hustle economy, she has become a popular guest on The Today Show, Business Insider, The Huffington Post, Forbes, Time, and other leading print and broadcast media outlets.

She is also a regular contributor to Fortune.com, Inc., Greatist, Brit + Co, and others.

susie-moore.com IG @susie.moore

more about

WHAT IF IT DOES WORK OUT?

- Do you have a hobby or passion that has nothing to do with your nine-to-five job? Do you craft vintage jewelry, make handmade furniture, or offer expert negotiating advice to family and friends in your spare time?
- Then you, too, could join the one-third of Americans who turn their talents into a lucrative side hustle.
- In What If It Does Work Out? life coach and professional side-hustler Susie Moore offers expert tips and guidance to help you earn an extra source of income by doing something you love.
- In her energetic and encouraging style, she guides you through all of the planning stages and potential obstacles, showing how to overcome any hesitation or fear, create multiple revenue streams, and more.
- Susie also presents inspiring stories from fellow side hustle successes, including the founders of Spanx and MindBodyGreen.
- Recommended by Entrepreneur magazine as a book "entrepreneurs must read to dominate their industry", What If It Does Work Out? features all you need to take the practical steps toward living the life of your dreams.

WHAT OTHERS SAY:
You Have a Dream, or a Calling:
This is How to Make Your Dream Come True

I cannot recommend this book more highly.
After reading this book, I had a whole new perspective on life, on money, and on what makes me happy

This book changed my life and gave me the energy and tools that I needed to begin putting my side hustle idea into action.
Susie has become a household name for us.
I even convinced my husband to start a side hustle, too!

97
YOU ARE A BADASS
AUTHOR: JEN SINCERO
How to Stop Doubting Your Greatness and Start Living an Awesome Life

Amazon (US) star rating: 4.7 ★
Number of Amazon (US) reviews: 16,727
Published: 2013

About the author:
Jen Sincero is a #1 New York Times bestselling author, success coach and motivational cattle prod who's helped countless people transform their personal and professional lives via her products, speaking engagements, newsletters, seminars and books.
You Are a Badass has sold over three million copies, is available in thirty-plus languages, and has been on the NY Times bestseller list for over 4 years.
Her follow-up, You Are a Badass at Making Money: Master the Mindset of Wealth (2017), also a New York Times bestseller, is written with the same inimitable sass, down-to-earth humor and blunt practicality that made You Are a Badass an indomitable bestseller and Jen a celebrated voice in the world of self development.
It is based on her own transformation, from a frustrated forty year-old living in a converted garage watching tumbleweeds blow through her empty bank account, to a successful business owner traveling the world in style.
jensincero.com IG *@jensincero*

more about
YOU ARE A BADASS

- You are a badass is the self-help book for people who desperately want to improve their lives but don't want to get busted doing it.
- In this refreshingly entertaining how-to guide, bestselling author and world-traveling success coach, Jen Sincero, serves up 27 bitesized chapters full of hilariously inspiring stories, sage advice, easy exercises, and the occasional swear word, helping you to:
1. Identify and change the self-sabotaging beliefs and behaviors that stop you from getting what you want
2. Create a life you totally love.
3. And create it NOW, Make some damn money already. The kind you've never made before.
- By the end of You Are a Badass, you'll understand why you are how you are, how to love what you can't change, how to change what you don't love, and how to use The Force to kick some serious ass.

WHAT OTHERS SAY:

10/10 recommend. Loved this book. One year ago I read this book and it helped change my life. Who knew all I had to do was change my thoughts and everything would fall into place!

I love everything about this book. I've had my self doubt, depressed days, anxiety, struggled with obesity, lived paycheck to paycheck, and also had a time in my life I was just content and happy. This entire book tells the truth, you may not like it but it's the real deal. I laughed, and nodded my head in agreement on many pages and can't wait to buy and read it again.

98
YOU ARE A BADASS AT MAKING MONEY
AUTHOR: JEN SINCERO
Master the Mindset of Wealth

Amazon (US) star rating: 4.7 ★
Number of Amazon (US) reviews: 2,540
Published: 2018

About the author:

Jen Sincero is a #1 New York Times bestselling author, success coach and motivational cattle prod who's helped countless people transform their personal and professional lives via her products, speaking engagements, newsletters, seminars and books.

Her #1 New York Times bestseller, You Are a Badass: How to Stop Doubting Your Greatness and Start Living an Awesome Life (2013), has sold over three million copies, is available in thirty-plus languages, and has been on the NY Times bestseller list for over 4 years.

Her follow-up, You Are a Badass at Making Money: Master the Mindset of Wealth (2017), also a New York Times bestseller, is written with the same inimitable sass, down-to-earth humor and blunt practicality that made You Are a Badass an indomitable bestseller and Jen a celebrated voice in the world of self development.

Based on her own transformation, from a frustrated forty year-old living in a converted garage watching tumbleweeds blow through her empty bank account, to a successful business owner traveling the world in style, You Are a Badass at Making Money is a testament to the fact that, in Jen's words: "If my broke ass can get rich, you can too."

jensincero.com   IG @jensincero

more about
YOU ARE A BADASS
AT MAKING MONEY

- You Are a Badass at Making Money will launch you past the fears and stumbling blocks that have kept financial success beyond your reach.
- Drawing on her own transformation—over just a few years—from a woman living in a converted garage with tumbleweeds blowing through her bank account to a woman who travels the world in style, Jen Sincero channels the inimitable sass and practicality that made You Are a Badass an indomitable bestseller.
- She combines hilarious personal essays with bite-size, aha concepts that unlock earning potential and get real results.
- Learn to:
- Uncover what's holding you back from making money
- Give your doubts, fears, and excuses the heave-ho
- Relate to money in a new (and lucrative) way
- Shake up the cocktail of creation
- Tap into your natural ability to grow rich
- Shape your reality—stop playing victim to circumstance
- Get as wealthy as you wanna be

WHAT OTHERS SAY:
"A cheerful manifesto on removing obstacles between yourself and the income of your dreams."
New York Magazine

"This book truly crystallizes the concept that financial abundance is an inside job—in that it all begins with your mindset—and Sincero gets serious (in the funniest ways possible) about helping you identify your particular limiting beliefs surrounding money." **PopSugar**

99
YOUR NEXT
FIVE MOVES

AUTHOR: PATRICK BET-DAVID

Master the Art of Business Strategy

Amazon (US) star rating: 5 ★
Number of Amazon (US) reviews: 750
Published: 2020

About the author:

Patrick Bet-David went from escaping war-torn Iran to founding his own financial services firm, raising tens of millions of dollars, and creating Valuetainment, the leading YouTube channel for entrepreneurs.
His unorthodox approach to business as well as life has led to compelling interviews with Ray Dalio, Kevin Hart, the late Kobe Bryant, President George W. Bush, and a host of other luminaries.
His content on social media has been viewed over a billion times.
Patrick never obtained a college degree and went from the army to selling health club memberships before entering the field of financial services.
At age thirty, he founded PHP, a financial services agency. He lives in Dallas with his wife and three children.

patrickbetdavid.com   *IG @patrickbetdavid*

more about
YOUR NEXT FIVE MOVES

- Both successful entrepreneurs and chess grandmasters have the vision to look at the pieces in front of them and anticipate their next five moves.
- In this book, Patrick Bet-David translates this skill into a valuable methodology that applies to high performers at all levels of business.
- Whether you feel like you've hit a wall, lost your fire, or are looking for innovative strategies to take your business to the next level, Your Next Five Moves has the answers.
- You will gain:
  1. CLARITY on what you want and who you want to be.
  2. STRATEGY to help you reason in the war room and the board room.
  3. GROWTH TACTICS for good times and bad.
  4. SKILLS for building the right team based on strong values.
  5. INSIGHT on power plays and the art of applying leverage.
- Combining these principles and revelations drawn from Patrick's own rise to successful CEO.

WHAT OTHERS SAY:

Wow... I can honestly say that this book just changed my life., how I look at life as a whole and how I make choices and how they affect others, in both business and life in general.

It even made me understand how I have let my PTSD take over and make choices for me. and I didn't even notice it.

Definitely reading it again.

Hands down, the best book I've read on business strategy

100
ZERO TO ONE
AUTHOR: PETER THIEL

A new way of thinking about innovation: it starts by learning to ask the questions that lead you to find value in unexpected places.

Amazon (US) star rating: 4.6 ★
Number of Amazon (US) reviews: 6,250
Published: 2014

About the author:

Peter Thiel is an entrepreneur and investor.
He started PayPal in 1998, led it as CEO, and took it public in 2002, defining a new era of fast and secure online commerce.
In 2004 he made the first outside investment in Facebook, where he serves as a director.
The same year he launched Palantir Technologies, a software company that harnesses computers to empower human analysts in fields like national security and global finance.
He has provided early funding for LinkedIn, Yelp, and dozens of successful technology startups, many run by former colleagues who have been dubbed the "PayPal Mafia."
He is a partner at Founders Fund, a Silicon Valley venture capital firm that has funded companies like SpaceX and Airbnb.
He started the Thiel Fellowship, which ignited a national debate by encouraging young people to put learning before schooling, and he leads the Thiel Foundation, which works to advance technological progress and long- term thinking about the future.

Blake Masters was a student at Stanford Law School in 2012 when his detailed notes on Peter's class "Computer Science 183: Startup" became an internet sensation. He is President of The Thiel Foundation and Chief Operating Officer of Thiel Capital.

more about
ZERO TO ONE

- The great secret of our time is that there are still uncharted frontiers to explore and new inventions to create. In Zero to One, legendary entrepreneur and investor Peter Thiel shows how we can find singular ways to create those new things.
- Thiel begins with the contrarian premise that we live in an age of technological stagnation, even if we're too distracted by shiny mobile devices to notice.
- Information technology has improved rapidly, but there is no reason why progress should be limited to computers or Silicon Valley.
- Progress can be achieved in any industry or area of business.
- It comes from the most important skill that every leader must master: learning to think for yourself.
- Doing what someone else already knows how to do takes the world from 1 to n, adding more of something familiar.
- But when you do something new, you go from 0 to 1.
- The next Bill Gates will not build an operating system. The next Larry Page or Sergey Brin won't make a search engine. Tomorrow's champions will not win by competing ruthlessly in today's marketplace.
- They will escape competition altogether, because their businesses will be unique.

WHAT OTHERS SAY:

Zero to One is the first book any working or aspiring entrepreneur must read—period.

Peter Thiel shows us that unconventional thinking (i.e. zero to one), is absolutely required to succeed with a new business.

Conventional thinking (for instance that competition is unavoidable (if you have something proprietary a la apple, it IS AVOIDABLE) , that competition is wonderful and necessary {but actually it is NOT}), is the linear approach (go from 1 to 1.1).

Conventional means copy others and when you do that you have to compete mainly by cutting prices. The leading businesses truly innovate (and everyone else follows or stay behind).

FROM THE AUTHOR:

I'm updating the book on a regular basis, and would love your feedback and input on books which made an impact on you or your business.
hello@abookamonth.club

And for the latest on everything business and self-development book related - let's connect
IG @abookamonth_by_marike
www.abookamonth.club

If this book helped you in any way, it will be lovely if you could write an Amazon review.
It really helps so much to
get the book to more people.

Sending the magic of books your way,
x Marike

keep track of other books you read

BOOKS LIST

Date	Book Title

keep track of other books you read

BOOKS LIST

Date	Book Title

a well read woman is a dangerous creature

Lisa Kleypas

hello@abookamonth.club

IG @abookamonth_by_marike

www.abookamonth.club

x Marike Fichardt

Printed in Great Britain
by Amazon